Typografische Grundlagen:
Gestaltung mit Schrift

Basic Typography:
Design with Letters

Ruedi Rüegg

VAN NOSTRAND REINHOLD
New York

Basic Typography: Design with Letters.

Typografische Grundlagen: Gestaltung mit Schrift.

Inhalt

Contents

Published in the U.S.A. by
Van Nostrand Reinhold
115 Fifth Avenue
New York, New York 10003

Distributed in Canada by
Macmillan of Canada
Division of Canada Publishing Corporation
164 Commander Boulevard
Agincourt, Ontario M1S 3C7, Canada

16 15 14 13 12 11 10 9 8 7 6 5 4 3 2 1

ISBN 0 442-23913-0

Beiträge von / Contributions of:
Claus Bremer
Giulio Cittato
Jürg Fritzsche
Takenobu Igarashi
Robert Krügel-Durband
Frans Lieshout (Total Design)
Hans-Rudolf Lutz
Pierre Mendell
Bruno Monguzzi
Siegfried Odermatt
Paul Rand
Rosmarie Tissi
Heinz Waibel
Wolfgang Weingart

Redaktionelle Mitarbeit / Editorial Assistance:
John Burbach
Übersetzung / Translation:
Andrew Bluhm (E)
Ruedi Bähler (D, S. 130, 134, 142, 154, 162, 166)

Gestaltung / Layout: Ruedi Rüegg, Zürich
Fotolithos / Color separations:
Cliché + Litho AG, Zürich
Titelsatz und Typoseiten / Special type pages
and titlesetting: Partnersatz, Bern
Gesamtherstellung / Production:
Jean Frey Druck, Zürich

Gedruckt in der Schweiz / Printed in Switzerland

Typografische Grundlagen: Gestaltung mit Schrift

Basic Typography: Design with letters

Die Praxis zeigt es täglich. Wir produzieren immer mehr visuell verbale Information. Wir bedrucken eine Unmenge Papier und entwickeln Programme für jegliche Art von Bildschirm. Wir sprechen von einer Informationsflut, einer Herausforderung für jeden typografischen Gestalter.

Warum das so ist, kann nicht das Thema dieses Handbuchs sein. Wie aber verbale Informationen ihrem Inhalt und Stellenwert entsprechend organisiert und gestaltet werden, in welcher Form diese die Empfänger erreichen, das ist unser Anliegen.

Der Begriff Typografie wird in dieser Schrift für die Gesamtheit des Bereichs visuelle Kommunikation mit Schrift verwendet. So bezeichnen wir zum Beispiel die Gestaltung eines Buches mit Satzschrift (Mengensatz) wie auch die Gestaltung eines Plakates mit Handschrift als Typografie. Worte verstehen wir zunächst als Inhalt, dann als Form und Technik. Typografie in diesem Sinn beschränkt sich in der Folge auf das rein Visuelle, auf das, was der Gestalter als Aufgabe zu lösen hat, das heisst, was er schliesslich den Lesern vorsetzt.

Seit Gutenberg hat sich die Satzproduktionstechnik in verschiedenen Entwicklungsstufen verändert, erneuert, verbessert. Die Schriftformen entstanden aber mehrheitlich nach von der Technik unabhängigen Kriterien (Zeitgeist, Architektur, industrielle Fortschritte usw.). Die Schriftgestalter jeder Epoche schufen die neuen Schriftformen primär im Einklang mit der ästhetischen Überzeugung ihrer Zeit. Das gleiche gilt für die Gestaltung der Drucksachen.

Bis vor nicht allzulanger Zeit war der Setzer mehrheitlich auch der Gestalter. Gestaltung und Produktion kamen aus einer Hand. Anfang des 20. Jahrhunderts übernahmen dann teilweise die Typografen und Grafiker, welche entweder aus dem Setzerberuf kamen oder sich durch entsprechende Ausbildung

It is a matter of daily experience that more and more visual verbal information is being produced all the time. Vast quantities of paper are printed, and programs are written for every kind of visual display terminal. We are witnessing a flood of information, which presents a challenge to every typographical designer.

The reasons why this should be so cannot be the theme of the present handbook. Our concern is with the methods of organizing and designing verbal information in accordance with its content and context and with the forms of publication in which this information is received by the reader.

We take the term "typography" to cover the entire spectrum of visual communication with script, including, for example, both the typographic design of books for the setting of large quantities of text and the hand-lettering design of a poster. We understand words as content in the first place, then as matters of form and technique. Typography in this sense is consequently limited to the purely visual, to the material on which the typographer must work in order to create an end-product that is placed before the reader.

Since Gutenberg's time the techniques of typesetting production have been changed, renewed and improved in various stages of development, while the forms of the typefaces have generally followed criteria which are independent of technique: the artistic style of the times, as also expressed in architecture, the progress of industry, and so on.

Until not too long ago, the typesetter was in most cases also the designer. Design and production came from one hand. Then, in the early years of the 20th century, the design function began to be taken over by typographers and graphic artists, who were either former typesetters or had obtained the necessary technical knowledge through appropriate training. Nowadays the situation is

die notwendigen Fachkenntnisse aneigneten, die Entwurfsarbeiten. Heute jedoch sind die satztechnischen Vorgänge derart komplex, dass der Gestalter mit Vorteil einen Berater zur Seite hat. Für die Zukunft zeichnet sich eine ähnliche Situation wie nach Gutenberg ab: Der Gestalter entwirft am Bildschirm und übermittelt mit dem Computer die reproduktionsbereiten Resultate. Und wieder kommt alles aus einer Hand.

Mit welcher Technik auch immer typografische Werke entstehen, sie sind nur so gut wie der Gestalter, der sie entwirft. Technik allein bürgt nie für formale Qualität, so hochentwickelt sie auch sein mag. Die Zukunft verlangt gut ausgebildete, kreative Gestalter, die neuen Problemstellungen gewachsen sind. Dieses Handbuch ist ein Hilfsmittel für die Ausbildung typografischer Gestalter. Es serviert keine Rezepte, vermittelt aber die wichtigsten Grundlagen für jede typografische Arbeit. Wenn es gelingt, Studenten und praktizierende Gestalter zu selbständigem, systematischem und fantasievollem Entwerfen anzuregen, ist das Ziel erreicht.

«Die Typografie ist einem eindeutigen Zweck verpflichtet, und zwar der schriftlichen Mitteilung. Durch kein Argument und durch keine Überlegung kann die Typografie von dieser Verpflichtung entbunden werden. Das Druckwerk, das nicht gelesen werden kann, wird zu einem sinnlosen Produkt.» Emil Ruder, 1967

Die Beispiele aus der Praxis zeigen, was auf einer soliden Basis entstehen kann.

different in that the technical processes of typesetting have become so complex that it is in the designer's interest to use the services of a technical consultant. For the future, a situation similar to that of the earliest years of typesetting can be foreseen, in that the designer will work at a display terminal, transmitting the repro-ready results via the computer, so that once again everything will come from one hand.

Whatever the techniques that may be used for typographical work, they can only be as good as the designer who uses them. Technique alone, however highly developed, can never guarantee aesthetic quality. The future calls for well-trained, creative designers, capable of handling the new kinds of problems that will arise.

The present handbook is intended as an aid to the training of typographical designers. It does not provide any ready-made answers but explains the most important basic requirements for all kinds of typographical work. If it succeeds in stimulating students and practising designers to produce original, systematic and imaginative work, it will have achieved its aim.

"Typography is devoted to a clear purpose, which is to convey meaning through the use of type. It cannot be exempted from this obligation by any kind of argument or any other consideration. The printed product that cannot be read has no meaning whatsoever." Emil Ruder, 1967

Our examples from commercial practice show what can be achieved on the basis of hard and fast groundwork.

Handwerk und Kunst
von Paul Rand

Craft and Art
by Paul Rand

Die Vorstellung, dass Intuition und Intellekt einander nicht ergänzen, dürfte längst überholt sein. Auf ähnlichen falschen Überlegungen beruht die Annahme, dass Inspiration handwerkliches Können und Wissen erübrige. Im Gegensatz dazu hat sich die Erkenntnis durchgesetzt, dass es für das künstlerische Schaffen von ausschlaggebender Bedeutung ist, sich mit den handwerklichtechnischen Grundregeln, im Sinne des Rohmaterials, vertraut zu machen.

Auf dem Gebiet des Graphic Design wie in allen Bereichen kreativer Tätigkeit wird die künstlerische Fähigkeit im wesentlichen auf die Beherrschung des Handwerks* zurückgeführt, auf das berufliche Metier, die Fachkenntnis. Beim Tanz zum Beispiel ist es unerlässlich, die Grundbegriffe des Schreitens, der rhythmischen Bewegung zu kennen. In der Musik ist die Kenntnis der Tonleitern lebensnotwendig. In der Typografie gehört die Beherrschung der Terminologie und die Erfassung ihres Sinnes zum fachlichen Rüstzeug. Der Typograf muss die Begriffe Punkt, Linie, Fläche, Durchschuss, Buchstabe, Wort, Pagina, Schriftzug, Papier, Druckfarbe, Druckverfahren, Buchbindereitechnik usw. kennen. Das Formen-Vokabular beinhaltet unter anderem Zwischenraum (Spatium), Abfolge, Serie, Bewegung, Gleichgewicht, Volumen, Spannung, Harmonie, Ordnung und Einfachheit.

So, wie es keine Kunst ohne Handwerk und kein Handwerk ohne Grundbegriffe gibt, ist Kunst ohne Phantasie, ohne Ideenflug nicht denkbar. Kindliche Kunst beruht auf starker Phantasie und relativ geringem handwerklichem Können. Erst die Intensität in der Verbindung von Einfallsreichtum und Technik schafft hier die feinen Unterschiede.

There is an old romantic idea that intuition and intellect do not mix. There is an equally erroneous belief that inspiration takes the place of industry. Fortified with such misconceptions, it is understandable that we tend to minimize the importance of learning the rules, the fundamentals, which are the raw material of the artist's craft.

In graphic design, as in all creative expression, art evolves from craft*. In dancing, craft is mastering the basic steps; in music, it is learning the scales. In typographic design, craft deals with points, lines, planes, picas, ciceros, leads, quads, serifs, letters, words, folios, pages, signatures, paper, ink, color, printing, and binding. The vocabulary of form (art) includes, among others: space, proportion, scale, size, shape, rhythm, repetition, sequence, movement, balance, volume, contrast, harmony, order, and simplicity.

Just as there is no art without craft and no craft without rules, so too there is no art without fantasy, without ideas. A child's art has much fantasy but little craft. It is the fusion of the two that makes the difference.

Freedom is the product of restraint (rules) which forms the basis for play and invention. If in a successful work a rule is or seems to be broken, one will discover that a compensatory element is operating: either an ingenious interpretation of a familiar rule or replacement of the rule with an extraordinary or novel element.

The history of art is also part of the artist's craft. It reveals the origin of the rules. Without the awareness of Burckhardt and Wölfflin, of Updike and Morison, the designer is

* Das Missverständnis, hervorgerufen durch die Bezeichnung «Arts and Crafts» (Kunst und Handwerk), hat die Kunst dem Handwerk entfremdet. Vielleicht kommt es daher, dass durch die Verbindung in der Bezeichnung «Handicraft» das Wort einen völlig anderen Sinn bekommen hat.

* The confusion that the phrase "arts and crafts" engenders has further alienated art from craft. Because of its association with handicrafts, the simple and the rustic, this combination of words has taken on quite another meaning.

Künstlerische Freiheit ist das Ergebnis erfasster und erlebter Gestaltungsprinzipien, die die Grundlage eines Zusammenwirkens von Spiel und Erfindung bilden. Werden in einem erfolgreichen Kunstwerk gewisse Gundsätze ausser acht gelassen, dann finden wir an ihrer Stelle kompensatorische Elemente: eine neue Interpretation der an sich bekannten Regeln oder den Ersatz durch ein aussergewöhnliches, neues Element.

Zur Geschichte der Kunst gehört unter anderem die Entwicklung des künstlerischen Handwerks und Könnens. Sie weist den Ursprung der Regeln nach. Ohne die Kenntnis von Burckhardts oder Wölfflins Theorien, derjenigen von Updike oder Morison wäre das Design ärmer. Kunstgeschichte offenbart die Beziehung von Picasso zu Masaccio, von Cézanne und den grossen Primitiven. Sie zieht die Grenzlinien zwischen Malewitsch und Lissitzky, macht deutlich, dass eine grössere Verwandtschaft besteht zwischen Mondrian und dem Swiss Design als zwischen dem Biedermeier und dem Bauhaus.

Gutes Design, gute Typografie, schweizerischen oder anderen Ursprungs, ist eine Verbindung von Information und Inspiration des Bewusstseins und Unterbewusstseins, von gestern und heute, von Realität und Phantasie, Arbeit und Spiel, Handwerk und Kunst.

all the poorer. Art history reveals the relationship of Picasso to Masaccio, to Cézanne and the primitives. It fixes the time between Malevich and Lissitzky. It suggests that without Mondrian, Swiss design might be more akin to Biedermeier than to Bauhaus.

Good design, good typography, Swiss or otherwise, is a fusion of information and inspiration, of the conscious and the unconscious, of yesterday and today, of fact and fantasy, work and play, craft and art.

(Freie deutsche Übertragung durch Hans Neuburg, Zürich)

Die folgende Übersicht zeigt die Entwicklung der lateinischen Schriftformen in ihren wichtigsten Phasen, angefangen bei der griechischen Lapidarschrift bis zu den in jüngster Zeit entwickelten Formen.

Die Zeitangaben beziehen sich auf die Perioden, in denen die Schriften angewandt wurden, oder auf deren Erscheinungsdatum.

Je nach Produktionstechnik und Quelle wurden Reproduktionen nach Originalen aus der Entstehungszeit oder aus der folgenden Anwendungsperiode verwendet (handgeschriebene Texte oder gezeichnete und dann geschnittene und gedruckte Schriften) wie auch nach später aufgezeichneten Schriften (zum Beispiel für die in Stein gehauenen Typen).

The following survey illustrates the principal stages in the development of roman letterforms, from ancient Greek inscriptions on stone to recently designed typefaces.

The dates given refer either to the periods during which the styles were generally used or to the year of their first appearance.

Depending on the sources of the originals and the techniques used for their production, the illustrations are taken either from the time of their introduction or period of current use, as in the case of handwritten texts and types drawn and subsequently cut for printing, or from lettering produced at a later time, for example certain scripts carved in stone.

5. Jahrhundert v. Chr. 5th century BC	Griechische Lapidarschrift Greek lapidary type	ATODANAKAT
2. Jahrhundert v. Chr. 2nd century BC	Römische Lapidarschrift Roman lapidary type	CORNELIVS·L
1. Jahrhundert v. Chr. 1st century BC	Römische Kapitalis Monumentalis Roman capitalis monumentalis	MATRONIS·
1. bis 5. Jahrhundert 1st to 5th century AD	Kapitalis rustika Capitalis rustica	BIT·ÁRCUMSU
1. bis 3. Jahrhundert 1st to 3rd century	Römische Majuskelkursiv Roman majuscule cursive	
3. bis 9. Jahrhundert 3rd to 9th century	Römische Unziale Roman uncial	CUIUSOBITU
3. bis 7. Jahrhundert 3rd to 7th century	Römische Minuskelkursiv Roman minuscule cursive	
3. bis 7. Jahrhundert 3rd to 7th century	Römische Halbunziale Roman half-uncial	&quia omne
4. und 5. Jahrhundert 4th and 5th century	Kapitalis quadrata Square capitals	CORNIBIN
7. bis 12. Jahrhundert 7th to 12th century	Irisch-angelsächsische Halbunziale Irish-Anglo-Saxon half-uncial	Zachariae-&salu
7. bis 9. Jahrhundert 7th to 9th century	Römische halbkursive Minuskel Roman half-cursive	uulnerre Conr
7. bis 9. Jahrhundert 7th to 9th century	Langobardische Minuskel Lombardic minuscule	R̄

7. und 8. Jahrhundert 7th and 8th century	Merowingische Minuskel Merovingian minuscule	
8. bis 11. Jahrhundert 8th to 11th century	Westgotische Minuskel Visigothic minuscule	
8. bis 11. Jahrhundert 8th to 11th century	Karolingische Minuskel Carolingian minuscule	
9. bis 13. Jahrhundert 9th to 13th century	Beneventanische Minuskel Beneventan minuscule	
11. und 12. Jahrhundert 11th and 12th century	Spätkarolingische Minuskel Late Carolingian minuscule	
12. und 13. Jahrhundert 12th and 13th century	Frühgotische Minuskel Early gothic minuscule	
13. bis 15. Jahrhundert 13th to 15th century	Gotische Minuskel Gothic minuscule	
13. bis 15. Jahrhundert 13th to 15th century	Gotische Kursiv (Bastarda) Gothic cursive (bastard)	
13. bis 15. Jahrhundert 13th to 15th century	Rotunda	
14. und 15. Jahrhundert 14th and 15th century	Textur Textura	
14. Jahrhundert 14th century	Gotico Antiqua Gotico antique	
15. und 16. Jahrhundert 15th and 16th century	Humanistische Minuskel Humanistic minuscule	

15. und 16. Jahrhundert 15th and 16th century	Humanistische Kursiv Humanistic cursive	*A t magnum fecit qu*
16. Jahrhundert 16th century	Schwabacher	Sertorius in de
16. und 17. Jahrhundert 16th and 17th century	Fraktur Fraktur (German type)	Zum erſten mach
16. Jahrhundert 16th century	Deutsche Kanzlei- und Kurrentschrift German chancery and running hand	nach Sant vlrichß f
1531	Garamond	ABCDE abcde
1725	Caslon	ABCDE abcde
Mitte 18. Jahrhundert Mid-18th century	Baskerville	ABCDE abcde
Mitte 18. Jahrhundert Mid-18th century	Fournier	ABCDE abcde
Mitte 18. Jahrhundert Mid-18th century	Didot	ABCDE abcde
1788 (1818)	Bodoni	ABCDE abcde
1803	Walbaum	ABCDE abcde
1816	Erste Groteskschrift First sans-serif	LETTERFOU

1821	Italienne	**ABCDEF**	
1844	Clarendon	**ABCD**	**abcd**
1898	Akzidenzgrotesk	ABCD	abcde
1927	Gill	ABCD	abcde
1927	Futura	ABCD	abcde
1931	Times New Roman	ABCD	abcde
1954	Folio	ABCD	abcde
1957	Univers	ABCD	abcd
1958	Helvetica	ABCD	abcde
1963	OCR-B	ABCD	abcd
1970	Frutiger	ABCD	abcde
1988	Rotis	ABCD	abcde

Obschon wir unter Typografie die Gesamtheit des Bereichs visuelle Kommunikation mit Schrift verstehen (das heisst die Verwendung von Satzschrift wie auch von individuell gestalteter Schrift), behandeln wir in der Folge nur die Elemente der industriell hergestellten Schriften, das heisst

- die Schriftformen
- die einzelnen Buchstaben
- das Wort
- die Zeile
- die Spalte
- die Linien, Zeichen und Symbole

Jeder Entwicklung einer persönlichen, künstlerischen Typografie liegen die elementaren Grundkenntnisse der typografischen Basis zugrunde.

Als unentbehrliches Hilfsmittel für die Gestaltung mit Schrift braucht jeder Typograf detaillierte Informationen über das ganze Schriftangebot seiner Schriftlieferanten (Setzerei/Druckerei). Diese Schriftmusterbücher sind bei den Schriftherstellern (zum Beispiel Berthold AG Berlin, Linotype Frankfurt, ITC New York, Mergenthaler New York, Haas'sche Schriftgiesserei Münchenstein [Schweiz] u.a.) und bei grossen Druckereien erhältlich. Die zum Teil umfassenden Werke zeigen alle erhältlichen Schrifttypen in allen Grössen, mit verschiedenem Duktus (Schriftlaufweiten), mit verschiedenen Zeilenabständen und geben die notwendigen Informationen über die entsprechende Satztechnik wie auch über die Art der Satzbestellung.

Jeder Gestalter sollte über eine sorgfältig ausgewählte Schriftmustersammlung verfügen.

Although our definition of typography covers the entire field of visual communication with letters, including the use of individually designed scripts as well as printing type, the following section is concerned only with the elements of industrially produced typefaces, viz:

- typeface forms
- the individual letters
- the word
- the line
- the column
- rules, signs and symbols

Every development of a personal, artistic typographical style is founded on a knowledge of the basic elements of typography.

As an indispensable aid to designing with type, every typographer needs detailed information on the entire typeface range of the supplier, whether typesetting service or printing company. Type-specimen books are available from leading printers and from type-manufacturing companies such as Berthold AG of Berlin, Mergenthaler Linotype of New York, Linotype Frankfurt and Cheltenham (England), ITC New York, Haas Typefoundry of Münchenstein, Switzerland, and many others. Comprehensive publications of this kind show all the available typefaces in all commonly used sizes, with a selection of letterspacing and leadings (inter-line spacing), and give the necessary information about the typesetting technique concerned and the prodedures for ordering setting.

Every typographic designer should have access to a carefully selected collection of type specimens.

Wir unterscheiden zwei Hauptgruppen der Druckschriften.

1.	Die Schriften mit Endstrichen (Serifen), zum Beispiel Bodoni, Times, Clarendon usw.

2.	Die Schriften ohne Endstriche, zum Beispiel Futura, Helvetica, Frutiger usw.

In einer dritten, jedoch sehr kleinen Gruppe von Satzschriften werden die Schreibschriften zusammengefasst, zum Beispiel Berthold Script, Englische Schreibschrift, Commercial Script usw.

In Europa besteht eine Klassifikation der Schriftformen, die 9 Gruppen unterscheidet. Diese feinere Gliederung hat jedoch wissenschaftlichen Charakter und ist eher für spezielle Studien von Nutzen (DIN-Norm 16518, 1964; British Standards 2961, 1967).

Das Schriftangebot heute ist quantitativ gewaltig; noch nie standen dem Gestalter so viele Formen zur Verfügung. Nach einer kritischen Betrachtung und sorgfältigen Auswahl stellen wir jedoch fest, dass nur eine geringe Zahl der Schriftformen den qualitativen Ansprüchen genügt, die wir zur Lösung von typografischen Aufgaben heute stellen müssen. Es ist auch richtig, dass wir Gestalter für unsere Arbeit mit wenigen, aber guten Schriftformen ohne weiteres auskommen. Denn wir haben die Aufgabe, dem Leser das Lesen zu vereinfachen, das Verstehen zu erleichtern. Weniger ist mehr!

Bei der Wahl der Schriftform ist primär darauf zu achten, für welchen Inhalt und Zweck wir diese einsetzen. Für umfangreiche Texte, zum Beispiel jede Art von Büchern, ist in der Regel nur eine, für den Mengensatz bewährte Schriftform zu verwenden (zum Beispiel Univers oder Times). Für besondere Fälle ist, wenn begründet, eine Mischung von zwei Schriftformen denkbar (zum Beispiel Times und Univers).

There are two main categories of printing typefaces.

1.	Those with serifs, e.g. Bodoni, Times, Clarendon, etc.

2.	Those without serifs, e.g. Futura, Helvetica, Frutiger, etc.

A third but very small group of printing typefaces comprises scripts, e.g. Berthold Script, English Script, Commercial Script, etc.

There is a European classification of type designs comprising 9 different groups, but these fine distinctions are more of an academic nature and are generally reserved for specialized studies (DIN standard 16518, 1964; British standard 2961, 1967).

An enormous variety of typefaces is available today, giving the designer a wider choice of forms than ever before; but after critical examination and careful selection we realize that only a small number of these typeface forms meet the qualitative requirements that we must put forward today for typographical work. Conversely, it is also quite right that we designers should be able to manage perfectly well in our work with few but well-designed typefaces, for our job is to make reading easier and to facilitate understanding. In this sense, less is more!

In choosing typeface forms the first considerations must be the content and the purpose of the matter concerned. As a rule, for extensive texts including all kinds of books, only one typeface of proven suitability for continuous matter (body copy) should be used. Univers or Times are prime examples. In special cases, where there is a good reason, a mixture of two typefaces is acceptable (e.g. Times with Univers).

Kurze Texte oder einzelne Worte jedoch, zum Beispiel für Buchumschläge oder Plakate, können sehr wohl nach freien, künstlerischen Gesichtspunkten gestaltet werden (mit Titelsatzschriften, gezeichneten Schriften usw.).

Die auf den folgenden Seiten gezeigten zwölf Schriftformen für den Mengensatz und Titel müssten für die Gestaltung der meisten typografischen Aufgaben genügen.

Die Alphabete sind in der Regel in den gebräuchlichen Satztechniken erhältlich, das heisst im Bleisatz (soweit noch vorhanden), im Fotosatz und teilweise im Schreibsatz.

Vorsicht: Der Name einer Schrift garantiert die formale Einheit der Schrift in den verschiedenen Satztechniken nicht. Wir stellen formale Unterschiede von Hersteller zu Hersteller fest.

Short texts or single words, on the other hand, e.g. for book jackets or posters, can certainly be designed freely by artistic standards, using headline faces or specially drawn characters, etc.

The 12 typeface forms for text setting and headlines shown on the following pages should suffice for the design of most typographical work.

As a rule the alphabets are available for the commonly used typesetting techniques, i.e. metal setting (where still in use), photosetting and, to a certain extent, typewriter setting.

Warning: The name of a typeface does not guarantee any conformity in the versions for different methods of setting. There are distinct differences between one manufacturer's version and another's.

Bodoni   Rockwell   Helvetica

Garamond
normal / regular

ABCDEFGHIJKLMNOPQRSTUVWXYZ
abcdefghijklmnopqrstuvwxyz
1234567890

Baskerville
normal / regular

ABCDEFGHIJKLMNOPQRSTUVWXYZ
abcdefghijklmnopqrstuvwxyz
1234567890

Bodoni
normal / regular

ABCDEFGHIJKLMNOPQRSTUVWXYZ
abcdefghijklmnopqrstuvwxyz
1234567890

Times
normal / regular

ABCDEFGHIJKLMNOPQRSTUVWXYZ
abcdefghijklmnopqrstuvwxyz
1234567890

Clarendon
mager / light

ABCDEFGHIJKLMNOPQRSTUVWXYZ
abcdefghijklmnopqrstuvwxyz
1234567890

Rockwell
normal / regular

ABCDEFGHIJKLMNOPQRSTUVWXYZ
abcdefghijklmnopqrstuvwxyz
1234567890

Akzidenzgrotesk
normal / regular

ABCDEFGHIJKLMNOPQRSTUVWXYZ
abcdefghijklmnopqrstuvwxyz
1234567890

Futura
normal / regular

ABCDEFGHIJKLMNOPQRSTUVWXYZ
abcdefghijklmnopqrstuvwxyz
1234567890

Gill
normal / regular

ABCDEFGHIJKLMNOPQRSTUVWXYZ
abcdefghijklmnopqrstuvwxyz
1234567890

Helvetica
normal / regular

ABCDEFGHIJKLMNOPQRSTUVWXYZ
abcdefghijklmnopqrstuvwxyz
1234567890

Univers
normal / regular

ABCDEFGHIJKLMNOPQRSTUVWXYZ
abcdefghijklmnopqrstuvwxyz
1234567890

Frutiger
normal / regular

ABCDEFGHIJKLMNOPQRSTUVWXYZ
abcdefghijklmnopqrstuvwxyz
1234567890

Der einzelne Buchstabe   **The Individual Letter**

Die Buchstaben sind die Einzelteile des ganzen Alphabets. Sie sind die Elemente, mit
denen Worte, Sätze und ganze Geschichten
«gebaut» werden. Die Buchstaben sind in
diesem Sinn die Bausteine der visuellen
Sprache. Diese Bausteine, so verschieden
sie auch in ihrer Form geliefert werden, sind
vorfabrizierte Teile, die wir in keiner Art und
Weise verändern. Das heisst auch, dass eine
8-Punkt-Schrift nicht auf 72 Punkt vergrössert oder eine Titelschrift beliebig verkleinert
werden darf. Die Resultate sind immer
schlecht.

As the component parts of the alphabet, letters are the elements with which words, sentences and whole stories are constructed. In
this sense, letters are the building-blocks of
speech made visible. Despite all the varieties
of form in which they are supplied, these
building-blocks are prefabricated components which we do not alter in any manner
or way. This has the consequence that an
8-point image should not be enlarged to 72
points, nor should a display face be reduced
in size at will: the results are always bad.

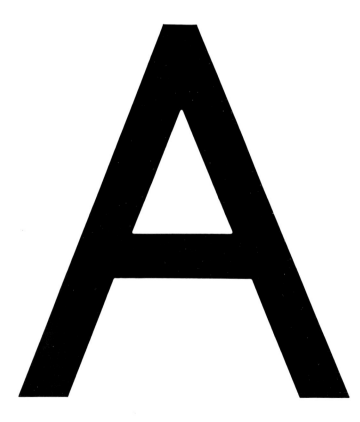

Univers-Alphabet, normal
Alphabet Univers, regular

Aa	Bb	Cc	Dd	Ee	Ff
Gg	Hh	Ii	Jj	Kk	Ll
Mm	Nn	Oo	Pp	Qq	Rr
Ss	Tt	Uu	Vv	Ww	Xx
Yy	Zz	Ää	Öö	Üü	
1	2	3	4	5	6
7	8	9	0		
. ,	: ;	– =	„ "	– +	*
! ?	( )	/ †	% §	$ £	&

Schriftschnitte

Das Schema der 22 aufeinander abgestimmten Schriftschnitte der Univers zeigt, was unter einem Schriftprogramm oder einer Schriftfamilie zu verstehen ist. Die von Adrian Frutiger gestaltete Schrift gibt dem Typografen unendlich viele Gestaltungsmöglichkeiten. Die Univers ist wohl auch deshalb eine der international erfolgreichsten Schriften.

Die meisten Schriften sind in einer kleineren oder grösseren Familie erhältlich. Üblich sind folgende Schriften: mager, normal, halbfett und fett. Dazu kommen die kursiven Schnitte und teilweise eine schmale Version. Ein umfassenderes Angebot ist eher selten.

Seite 25
Univers

von oben nach unten:

- leicht
- mager
- normal
- halbfett
- fett
- extrafett

Von links nach rechts:

- breit
- normal
- normal kursiv
- schmal
- schmal kursiv
- extraschmal

Type Styles

The illustration of the 22 related styles of Univers shows what is meant by a typeface series or family. Univers, designed by Adrian Frutiger, gives the typographer an immense range of design possibilities, which is probably another reason why it has been one of the most successful typefaces on an international scale.

Most typefaces are available in larger or smaller families. The following styles are common: light, roman (regular), medium and bold, together with the italic styles and in some cases a condensed version. A more extensive set of alternative styles is rather rare.

Page 25
Univers

from top to bottom:

- extra light
- light
- roman (regular)
- medium
- bold
- extra bold

From left to right:

- extended
- roman (regular)
- roman (regular) italic
- condensed
- condensed italic
- extra condensed

Schema der 22 aufein-
ander abgestimmten
Schnitte der Univers

Diagram of 22 type styles
of Univers,
adjusted to one another

Schriftstärken

Stärken nennt man die verschiedenen
Dicken der Striche im Verhältnis zu den
Innenräumen bei gleichbleibender Höhe.
Die Stärken werden gestuft in

- leicht
- mager
- normal
- halbfett
- fett
- extrafett

Eine einheitliche Normierung der Massverhältnisse existiert jedoch nicht. So ist zum
Beispiel fett bei der Univers nicht gleich fett
wie bei der Helvetica oder Gill.

Die magern und normalen Schnitte werden
vorwiegend für grössere Textmengen verwendet. Halbfette, fette und extrafette
Schnitte eignen sich besonders für Titel und
Auszeichnungen im Text.

Type Weights

The various thicknesses of stroke of a
typeface in relation to its interior spaces
(counters), without alteration of height, are
known as weights. They are graduated as

- extra light
- light
- roman (regular)
- medium
- bold
- extra bold

There is, however, no unified standardization
of the thickness ratio. Thus the black version
of Univers is not of the same weight as Helvetica Bold or the corresponding style of Gill
Sans.

The light and roman styles are predomi-
nantly used for large quantities of text setting. Medium, bold and extra-bold styles are
particularly suitable for headings and special
emphasis in the text.

H

H

H

H

H

Schriftbreiten

Unter Breiten verstehen wir, wie das Wort es sagt, die effektiven Breiten der Buchstaben. Die Breite eines Buchstabens steht in einem bestimmten Verhältnis zur Strichdicke und zum Innenraum bei gleichbleibender Höhe. Die Breiten werden gestuft in

– extraschmal
– schmal
– normal
– breit
– extrabreit

Wie bei den Stärken besteht auch im Bereich der Breiten keine einheitliche Normierung der Massverhältnisse. Jede Schriftfamilie hat ihre besonders abgestimmten Proportionen.

Für grosse Textmengen verwendet man mit Vorteil normale Schriftbreiten (optimale Lesbarkeit). Besondere Aufgaben rechtfertigen in Ausnahmefällen die schmalen oder breiten Schnitte.

Type Widths

This term refers to the effective width of the style of letter. The widths are in a definite relation to stroke thickness and counters, at an equal height, and are graduated as

– extra condensed
– condensed
– roman (regular)
– extended
– extra extended

As with weights, there is no unified standardization of ratios in the field of widths. Every typeface family has its own specially designed proportions.

For large quantities of text it is advantageous to use roman widths, designed for optimum legibility. In exceptional cases, special requirements sanction the use of condensed or expanded styles.

H

H

Schriftlagen

Als Ergänzung zu den geraden Schriften, also zu all denen, die im rechten Winkel zur Grundlinie stehen, sind kursive Schriften erhältlich. Kursive Schriften sind in einer Richtung geneigte Schriften.

Innerhalb eines gut ausgebauten Schriftprogramms besteht zu jeder geraden Buchstabenvariante eine kursive.

Kursive Schriften finden im Mengensatz wie auch für Auszeichnungen im Text und für Titel ihre Anwendung.

Angles of Slope

Italic typefaces are available as supplements to the upright faces, i.e. all those that stand at right angles to the baseline. Italics are sloped in one direction.

A well-equipped type library will include an italic style of every roman typeface.

Italics are used in continuous texts as well as for emphasis within a roman text and for headlines.

H
H
H
H
H
H
H
H
H
H
H
H
H
H
H
H

Schriftgrössen

Im Blei- und Fotosatz werden die Schriftgrössen in Punkten oder Millimetern angegeben. Diese Punktzahl ist als Name, nicht als messbare Grösse zu verstehen. Es ist zu beachten, dass dieses Mass nicht der Versalhöhe des Buchstabens entspricht, sondern der Höhe des Kegels im Bleisatz oder dem Mindestzeilenabstand im Fotosatz. Beispiel: 8 Punkt Bleisatzkegel entsprechen im Fotosatz einem Mindestzeilenabstand von 3 mm (Berthold).

Je nach Hersteller liegen die Schriftgrössen für den Mengensatz in der Regel zwischen 5 und 36 Punkt (im Bleisatz bis 72 Punkt, im Fotosatz zum Teil bis 360 Punkt, sogenannte Supertypegeräte haben einen Bereich von 4,5–90 mm).

Beispiel für die Grössenschritte (Berthold):

5 Punkt	13 Punkt	22 Punkt
6 Punkt	14 Punkt	24 Punkt
7 Punkt	15 Punkt	26 Punkt
8 Punkt	16 Punkt	28 Punkt
9 Punkt	17 Punkt	30 Punkt
10 Punkt	18 Punkt	32 Punkt
11 Punkt	19 Punkt	34 Punkt
12 Punkt	20 Punkt	36 Punkt

Für die praktische Arbeit mit Mengensatz ist ein gutes Schriftmusterbuch mit den entsprechenden Grössenangaben erforderlich. Nur der Vergleich mit den sichtbaren Beispielen ermöglicht die richtige Grössenwahl.

Titelsatz wird in Millimetern bestellt, das heisst zum Beispiel Versalhöhe 25 mm. Titelsatz kann je nach System von etwa 12 mm bis 50 mm geliefert werden.

Type Sizes

For metal setting and all kinds of photosetting, type sizes are given in points, inches or millimeters. The point size is to be understood as a denomination, not a measurable size, since it does not correspond to the capital height of the letter but to the body size of the metal type or the basic line depth in phototype. For example, an 8-point type-body size corresponds to a basic line depth of 3 mm in photosetting (Berthold).

Depending on the manufacturer, type sizes for continuous or "straight" setting generally range from 5 to 36 points. This range of standard sizes can go up to 72 points with hot-metal machines, and with photosetters in some cases to 360 points. "Supertype" equipment provides a range from 4.5 to 90 mm.

The Berthold range provides an example of type-size increments:

5 points	13 points	22 points
6 points	14 points	24 points
7 points	15 points	26 points
8 points	16 points	28 points
9 points	17 points	30 points
10 points	18 points	32 points
11 points	19 points	34 points
12 points	20 points	36 points

For practical purposes in composition, a good type-specimen book with the relevant size information is necessary. The right choice of type size is possible only by means of comparison of samples.

Display or headline setting is ordered in millimeter or inch measurements, e.g. a cap height of 25 mm or 1 inch. Depending on the system in use, display setting can be supplied in sizes from about 12 to 50 mm (0.05 to 2 inches).

Eine Hilfe für die Bestimmung der Schriftgrössen für Drucksachen sind die drei Funk-
tionsgruppen:

Lesegrössen:

- Schriftgrössen von 8 bis 12 Punkt
- Für Mengensatz (Haupttexte)
- Gut lesbar aus normaler Lesedistanz

Konsultationsgrössen:

- Schriftgrössen von 5 bis 8 Punkt
- Für Anmerkungen, Fussnoten, Bildlegen-
  den, Tabellen, Register, zum Teil auch für
  Nachschlagewerke
- Lesbar, da in der Regel nur kurze Texte

Titelgrössen:

- Schriftgrössen von 14 bis 36 Punkt im
  Mengensatz sowie die sogenannten
  Plakatschriftgrössen von 36 Punkt bis . . .
- Für Titel, Auszeichnungen, Signale
- Sehr gut lesbar, auch aus grosser Distanz
  (Plakate)

Schriftgrössen und Lesedistanzen
zum Beispiel für Plakate (Faustregel):

Buchstabengrösse	maximale Lesedistanz
20 mm	10 m
40 mm	20 m
60 mm	30 m
80 mm	40 m
100 mm	50 m

A further aid for the specification of type
sizes is provided by classification according
to function into three categories:

Text-type Sizes:

- Type sizes from 8 to 12 points.
- For straight setting of main texts.
- Clearly legible at normal reading distance.

Reference Sizes:

- Type sizes from 5 to 8 points.
- For notes, footnotes, captions, tables,
  listings, and to some extent for complete
  works of reference.
- Legible because the texts concerned are
  generally short.

Headline Sizes:

- Type sizes from 14 to 36 points for straight
  setting and large display or "poster" sizes
  from 36 points onward.
- For headlines, advertising display and road
  signs, etc.
- Outstandingly legible even from a distance
  (posters).

Type sizes and reading distances, e.g. for
posters (rule of thumb):

Type size		maximum reading distance
0.5	inch	20 ft
1	inch	40 ft
2	inches	80 ft
3	inches	120 ft
4	inches	160 ft

Wörter sind Kombinationen von Einzelbuchstaben, lesbar von links nach rechts.

Die Buchstabenfolge eines Wortes ist durch die Grammatik bestimmt. Wir kennen die Buchstabenformen. Unsere Aufgabe besteht darin, die Buchstaben entsprechend ihrer formalen Charakteristik im richtigen Abstand zueinander aufzureihen.

Zu unterscheiden ist nun allerdings, in welcher Technik die Schrift produziert wird, in welcher Grösse und für welchen Zweck.

Bei handelsüblichen Schriften für den *Mengensatz* (Blei- und Fotosatz) sind die Buchstabenabstände nach dem Prinzip der optimalen Lesbarkeit reguliert, das heisst, jede Kombination der Buchstaben zueinander wird durch das entsprechende System oder Programm automatisch ausgeglichen. Der Gestalter hat jedoch bei der Verwendung von Fotosatz die Wahl, die Schriftweite (Duktus, Buchstabenabstände) gesamthaft offener oder enger zu bestellen (je nach System in verschiedenen Schritten). Der Bleisatz kennt nur normale und offenere Schriftweiten.

Grundsätzlich hat sich für den Mengensatz in den meisten Systemen die normale Schriftweite bewährt. Enge Schriftweiten sind sehr schnell schlecht lesbar und deshalb nicht zu empfehlen.

Die Buchstabengrössen verhalten sich zu den Buchstabenabständen so, dass kleine Grade grössere Abstände benötigen und umgekehrt.

Words are combinations of single letters, reading from left to right.

The sequence of letters is determined by orthographic rules. We know the forms of the letters, and our job is to align them at the correct intervals in accordance with the characteristics of these forms.

Factors which must be taken into consideration are the technique of typesetting production, the size of the type and the purpose for which it is being used.

Normal commercial typefaces for *continuous matter or body copy* set in metal or on film have their distances between the letters regulated in accordance with the principles of optimum legibility, which means that every combination of letters is automatically spaced by the system or computer program concerned. At the same time, when using photosetting, the designer has the option of ordering an overall widening or narrowing of set-widths. This is achieved in a series of steps which will differ from one system to another. In metal setting, the only choices are normal and more open set-widths.

Normal set-widths have proved to be generally correct for continuous setting by most systems. A narrower set soon becomes hard to read and is therefore not recommendable.

Set-widths relate to type sizes in such a way that the smaller sizes need relatively greater widths, and vice versa.

sehr weit very loose	Schriftweiten	Schriftweiten
weit loos	Schriftweiten	Schriftweiten
normal	Schriftweiten	Schriftweiten
eng tight	Schriftweiten	Schriftweiten
zu eng too tight	Schriftweiten	Schriftweiten
sehr weit very loose	Letterspaces	Letterspaces
weit loose	Letterspaces	Letterspaces
normal	Letterspaces	Letterspaces
eng tight	Letterspaces	Letterspaces
zu eng too tight	Letterspaces	Letterspaces

rund round	ceos	COQS
vertikal vertical	il i hmnu	I HMNU
rund und vertikal round and vertical	abdgpq frt	BDGPR
vertikal und horizontal vertical and horizontal		EFLT
schräg oblique	vwxy	VWXY
schräg und vertikal/ horizontal oblique and vertical/ horizontal	kz	AKZ

Seite 32:
Gruppierung der
Buchstabenformen

Page 32:
Grouping of
letter shapes

Bei grösseren Schriftgraden, über 14 Punkt und *Titelschriften,* werden die durch die jeweilige Technik bedingten Unregelmässigkeiten sichtbar. Zu kleine oder zu grosse Zwischenräume verlangen eine Korrektur.

Um eine ungestörtes, flüssiges Lesen zu ermöglichen, suchen wir ein ruhiges, regelmässig rhythmisches Schriftbild zu erlangen. Wir schliessen störende Löcher und öffnen enge, dunkle Stellen.

With type sizes above 14 points, and with *display faces* the irregularities which are due to the technique in use become visible, calling for correction where the space between letters is too great or too small.

For easy and fluent reading we need to produce a tranquil type image with regular rhythm, closing up distracting gaps and opening up dark and narrow junctions.

Nicht ausgeglichene Buchstabenabstände
Unjustified letter spacing

Ausgeglichene Buchstabenabstände
Justified letter spacing

Typografie   Typografie

TYPOGRAF   TYPOGRAF

Legibility   Legibility

LEGIBILITY   LEGIBILITY

Die Zeile

The Line

Die Zeile besteht aus aneinandergereihten Wörtern. Zwischen den Wörtern liegt der Wortabstand. Der Wortabstand muss so dimensioniert sein, dass sich die einzelnen Wörter deutlich voneinander abheben. Zu grosse Wortabstände, das heisst zu grosse Leerräume (Löcher) stören den Lesefluss. Wir suchen also eine möglichst regelmässige Aneinanderreihung der Wörter.

Der Wortzwischenraum ist von der Schriftweite der Wörter abhängig. Für normale Schriftweiten im Mengensatz gilt folgende Faustregel: Wortzwischenraum = $\frac{1}{3}$ Geviert (Bleisatz) oder dem Innenraum des n entsprechende Anzahl Einheiten (Fotosatz). Diese Regel für die Wortabstände im regelmässig fortlaufenden Satz (Flattersatz) ist automatisch Bestandteil der Satzsysteme oder Programme und muss nicht speziell angefordert werden.

Wortzwischenräume bei grossen Schriften (Titelschriften) variieren je nach Form und Grösse. Hier werden Unregelmässigkeiten bei Verwendung gleicher Zwischenräume sichtbar. Je nach Form des letzten Buchstabens eines Wortes und des ersten des folgenden Wortes ist der Zwischenraum optisch auszugleichen.

The line consists of an alignment of words, with word space between them. Word space must be sufficient for a clear separation of each word from the next but not so great as to produce gaps which disturb the flow of reading. The aim is thus the most regular possible arrangement of words.

Word spacing is dependent upon the width of the word. The following rule of thumb applies for normal character widths in continuous matter: word space = $\frac{1}{3}$ em of the body size (metal) or equivalent units (photosetting). This rule for word spacing in regularly spaced (unjustified) matter is an automatic element of the typesetting system or program and does not have to be specially ordered.

With large type sizes (display faces), wordspacing varies according to the size and form of the letters. When exactly equal spacing is used, irregularities in the letterforms become apparent. The spacing must be optically equalized to suit the forms of the last letter of one word and the first letter of the next.

zu weit too loose	The　space　between　words
weit loose	The　space　between　words
offen open	The space between words
normal regular	The space between words
eng tight	The space between words
zu eng too tight	The space between words
kein Wortabstand no wordspace	Thespacebetweenwords

zu weit too loose	The　space　between　words
weit loose	The　space　between　words
offen open	The space between words
normal regular	The space between words
eng tight	The space between words
zu eng too tight	The space between words
kein Wortabstand no wordspace	Thespacebetweenwords

»Neue Typographie« als Schlagwort und als Titel hatte zur Zeit des Erscheinens von Tschicholds Buch schon Geschichte. ›Die Neue Typographie‹ war der Titel eines programmatischen Aufsatzes von Laszlo Moholy-Nagy im ›Bauhausbuch‹ 1923, das im Zusammenhang mit der ›Bauhaus-Ausstellung‹ in Weimar er-schienen ist, die auch Jan Tschichold umgekehrt hat. Moholy-Nagy fordert darin »zuallererst: eindeutige Klarheit in

Editors, printers, designers, ophthalmolo-gists, and educators have been concerned with the legibility of print for more than a century. In the earlier ears, there were many opinions and recommendations expressed on this subject; however, these were based on casual observation rather than upon research findings. Prior to 1900, there were very few experimental studies reported, but since 1925, research in the field has expanded markedly.

»Neue Typographie« als Schlagwort und als Titel hatte zur Zeit des Erscheinens von Tschicholds Buch schon Geschichte. ›Die Neue Typographie‹ war der Titel eines programmatischen Aufsatzes von Laszlo Moholy-Nagy im ›Bauhausbuch‹ 1923, das im Zusammenhang mit der ›Bauhaus-Aus-stellung‹ in Weimar erschienen ist, die auch Jan Tschichold umgekehrt hat. Moholy-Nagy fordert darin »zuallererst: eindeutige Klarheit in allen typographischen Werken.

Editors, printers, designers, ophthalmolo-gists, and educators have been concerned with the legibility of print for more than a century. In the earlier years, there were many opinions and recommendations expressed on this subject; however, these were based on casual observation rather than upon research findings. Prior to 1900, there were very few experimental studies reported, but since 1925, research in the field has expanded markedly. Befor the nineteenth century, the

»Neue Typographie« als Schlagwort und als Titel hatte zur Zeit des Erscheinens von Tschicholds Buch schon Geschichte. ›Die Neue Typographie‹ war der Titel eines programmatischen Aufsatzes von Laszlo Moholy-Nagy im ›Bauhausbuch‹ 1923, das im Zusammenhang mit der ›Bauhaus-Aus-stellung‹ in Weimar erschienen ist, die auch Jan Tschichold umgekehrt hat. Moholy-Nagy fordert darin »zuallererst: eindeutige Klarheit in allen typographischen Werken.

Editors, printers, designers, ophthalmologists, and educators have been concerned with the legibility of print for more than a century. In the earlier years, there were many opinions and recommendations expressed on this subject; however, these were based on casual observa-tion rather than upon research findings. Prior to 1900, there were very few experimental studies reported, but since 1925, research in the field has expanded markedly. Befor the nineteenth century, the main concern was with

Mr. John William Kim

Mr. John William Kim

DER FALL VON ANDREA

DER FALL VON ANDREA

Die Spalte

The Column

Eine Spalte nennt man eine grössere Anzahl von Zeilen untereinander in einer bestimmten Breite.

Die Spalte (Breite und Höhe) wird bestimmt durch

- die Anzahl der Buchstaben pro Zeile
- die Schriftgrösse
- den Zeilenabstand
- die Anzahl der Zeilen
- den verfügbaren Raum

Von Spalten sprechen wir hauptsächlich im Mengensatz. Die Praxis hat gezeigt, dass die Spaltenbreiten der meisten Imprimate (Zeitschriften, Broschüren) 5 bis 8 Wörter mit durchschnittlich 40 bis 60 Buchstaben enthalten, Tageszeitungen enthalten eher weniger, Bücher oft mehr Buchstaben pro Zeile. Auch wenn für die Anzahl der Buchstaben pro Zeile keine Normen bestehen, dürfen wir die Erfahrungszahl von 40 bis 60 Buchstaben als leicht lesbare Menge verwenden.

Bei der Wahl der Schriftgrösse im Mengensatz sind die Möglichkeiten schon eingeschränkt, das heisst, wir haben den Umfang des Textes, den zur Verfügung stehenden Raum, die Bedeutung des Inhalts und nicht zuletzt auch die Lesegewohnheiten der Empfänger (zum Beispiel Sehbehinderte, alte Leute oder Kinder) zu berücksichtigen.

Die Grössen im Mengensatz für die Grundschrift liegen zwischen 8 und 12 Punkt.

Den Zeilenabstand im Bleisatz ohne zusätzlichen Durchschuss (Leerraum) nennt man «kompress gesetzt» – im Fotosatz «Mindestzeilenabstand», welcher nie unterschritten werden darf, auch wenn die Fotosatztechnik dies ermöglicht.

In vielen Fällen ist aber zusätzlicher Durchschuss notwendig. In der Regel benötigen kurze Zeilen keinen oder wenig Durchschuss, lange Zeilen mehr. Gut durchschossene

A series of lines one under another makes a column of a given width.

Column width and height are determined by

- the number of characters per line
- the type size
- the distance between lines
- the number of lines
- the space available

The column is generally an element of continuous text or body copy. Practical experience has shown that the column widths of most printed matter (magazines, brochures) contain from 5 to 8 words, averaging 40 to 60 characters. Newspapers have fewer characters per line and books often have more. Even though there are no standards for the number of characters per line, we can take the average number of 40 to 60 characters as being an easily readable quantity.

There are already some limitations to the choice of type size for continuous matter, since we must take into account the length of the text, the space available, the nature of the content and, not least, the reading habits of the recipient, including short-sighted, elderly people and children.

Type sizes for continuous text matter are between 8 and 12 points.

Lines composed in metal without leading (interlinear spacing) are known as "solid setting". The corresponding term for photosetting is "minimum line depth", which should never be undercut, even though phototype technique makes this possible.

On the other hand, additional leading is necessary in many cases. Short lines generally need little or no leading, while long lines need more. Well-leaded lines emphasize the horizontal and make reading easier.

Zeilen betonen die horizontale Linie und erleichtern das Lesen. Der für eine bestimmte Aufgabe gewählte Zeilenabstand ermöglicht dann im vorgesehenen Format eine entsprechende Anzahl von Zeilen.

Je nach typografischer Arbeit (zum Beispiel Buch oder Ausstellungstafel) sind die Dimensionen eines gegebenen Formates massgeblich mitbestimmend für die Gestaltung der Spalte(n).

Nur in Abstimmung mit den genannten Rahmenbedingungen kann eine optimale Satzspalte definiert werden. Eine Spalte wirkt dann ruhig und ist angenehm und leicht zu lesen, wenn eine Einheit von Schriftweite, Wortabständen, Zeilenlängen und Zeilenabständen erreicht wird.

Bei mehreren Titelzeilen untereinander ist der Zeilenabstand dem Schriftbild optisch anzupassen. Hier wirkt unter Umständen gleichmässiger Zeilenabstand (Durchschuss) optisch ungleichmässig. Solche «Fehler» gleichen wir mit verschiedenen Zeilenabständen aus.

Choice of a given depth of line for a given job makes it possible to calculate in advance the number of lines to the required page size.

In each kind of work (e.g. book or display panel), the dimensions of the page size or format are an important factor in determining the arrangement of columns.

The ideal column dimensions can be defined only by taking into account these considerations. A column of type has a tranquil appearance and is easy and pleasant to read when a unity of set-width, word spacing, line length, and leading has been achieved.

Where display lines are placed one above another, the space between lines has to be judged optically. In some cases equal linespaces (leading) has an unequal optical effect. Such "errors" are overcome by different variations of linespacing.

Die Spaltenarten

Innerhalb einer gegebenen Spaltenbreite lassen sich die Zeilen auf vier verschiedene Arten anordnen

- Flattersatz links angeschlagen
- Flattersatz rechts angeschlagen
- Blocksatz
- symmetrisch auf die Mittelachse ausgerichteter Satz

Im Flattersatz links angeschlagen beginnen die Zeilen immer auf der linken Spaltenseite und laufen innerhalb der Spaltenbreite mit normalen Wortabständen frei nach rechts aus. Es ist darauf zu achten, dass die Zeilenenden trotzdem einen mehr oder weniger ruhigen Abschluss bilden. Vernünftige Trennungen der Wörter sind nicht verboten.

Rechts angeschlagener Flattersatz ist schwer zu lesen und soll nur in Ausnahmefällen verwendet werden.

Im Blocksatz ist die Zeile links und rechts der Spalte bündig. Der durch den Text bedingte Leerraum (Rest einer Zeile) wird pro Zeile gleichmässig zwischen den Wörtern verteilt. Das ergibt von Zeile zu Zeile verschiedene Wortabstände (Normalabstand plus Anteil vom Rest). Am ruhigsten wirkt der Blocksatz mit 50 und mehr Buchstaben pro Zeile. Je mehr Wörter, desto besser und gleichmässiger verteilen sich die Wortabstände. Mit wenig Wörtern entstehen schnell störende Löcher.

Mittelachsgruppierung heisst die symmetrische Anordnung der Zeilen auf die vertikale Mittelachse. Die Wortabstände sind in jeder Zeile gleich. Diese Spaltenform ist für lange Texte nicht zu empfehlen.

Kinds of Columns

Within a given column width, lines can be arranged in four different ways

- unjustified, range left
- unjustified, range right
- justified
- symmetrically centered

In unjustified setting, range left, the lines always begin on the left side of the column and run freely within the width of the column with normal spaces between the words. Care must be taken that the ends of the lines form an agreeable margin.

Unjustified setting, range right is difficult to read and should only be used in exceptional cases.

In justified setting, the lines are flush at the left and right of the column. The spaces occurring (the remainder of a line) are equally distributed between the words on each line. This means that the word spaces vary from line to line (normal space between words plus part of the remainder). Justified setting with 50 and more letters per line presents the most agreeable effect. The more words there are, the better and more regularly the spaces between the words can be distributed. Disturbing holes soon appear if there are only a few words.

Unjustified setting, centered, is the symmetrical arrangement of the lines on each side of the vertical axis. The distance between the words is the same on every line. This type of column is not recommended for long texts.

Flattersatz
links bündig
Unjustified setting
left binding

Flattersatz
rechts bündig
Unjustified setting
right binding

»Neue Typographie« als Schlagwort und
als Titel hatte zur Zeit des Erscheinens von
Tschicholds Buch schon Geschichte. ›Die
Neue Typographie‹ war der Titel eines
programmatischen Aufsatzes von Laszlo
Moholy-Nagy im ›Bauhausbuch‹ 1923, das
im Zusammenhang mit der ›Bauhaus-
Ausstellung‹ in Weimar erschienen ist, die
auch Jan Tschichold umgekehrt hat.
Moholy-Nagy fordert darin »zuallererst:
eindeutige Klarheit in allen typographischen Werken. Die Lesbarkeit – die Mitteilung darf nie unter einer a priori angenommenen Aesthetik leiden. Die Buchstabentypen dürfen nie in eine vorbestimmte

Editors, printers, designers, ophthalmologists, and educators have been concerned
with the legibility of print for more than a
century. In the earlier years, there were many
opinions and recommendations expressed on
this subject; however, these were based on
casual observation rather than upon research
findings. Prior to 1900, there were very few
experimental studies reported, but since
1925, research in the field has expanded
markedly. Before the nineteenth century, the
main concern was with esthetic appearance of
print. With improved technology of printing,
two additional factors entered the picture:
Economy of printing and traditional practi-

Blocksatz
Justified setting

Symmetrischer Satz
Symmetrical setting

»Neue Typographie« als Schlagwort und als
Titel hatte zur Zeit des Erscheinens von
Tschicholds Buch schon Geschichte. ›Die
Neue Typographie‹ war der Titel eines
programmatischen Aufsatzes von Laszlo
Moholy-Nagy im ›Bauhausbuch‹ 1923, das
im Zusammenhang mit der ›Bauhaus-
Ausstellung‹ in Weimar erschienen ist, die
auch Jan Tschichold umgekehrt hat.
Moholy-Nagy fordert darin »zuallererst:
eindeutige Klarheit in allen typographischen
Werken. Die Lesbarkeit – die Mitteilung darf
nie unter einer a priori angenommenen
Aesthetik leiden. Die Buchstabentypen
dürfen nie in eine vorbestimmte Form, z. B.

Editors, printers, designers,
ophthalmologists, and educators have been
concerned with the legibility of print
for more than a century. In the earlier years,
there were many opinions and
recommendations expressed on this subject;
however, these were based on
casual observation rather than upon research
findings. Prior to 1900, there were very
few experimental studies reported, but since
1925, research in the field has
expanded markedly. Before the nineteenth
century, the main concern was with
esthetic appearance of print. With improved

Buchstaben Characters	44	68	92
Zeilenlänge (mm) Length of lines (mm)	67,5	105	142,5

»Neue Typographie« als Schlagwort und als

»Neue Typographie« als Schlagwort und als Titel hatte zur Zeit des E

»Neue Typographie« als Schlagwort und als Titel hatte zur Zeit des Erscheinens von Tschicho

9 Punkt auf 3,5 mm
9 points on 3,5 mm

»Neue Typographie« als Schlagwort und
als Titel hatte zur Zeit des Erscheinens von
Tschicholds Buch schon Geschichte. ›Die
Neue Typographie‹ war der Titel eines

9 Punkt auf 3,75 mm
9 points on 3,75 mm

»Neue Typographie« als Schlagwort und
als Titel hatte zur Zeit des Erscheinens von
Tschicholds Buch schon Geschichte. ›Die
Neue Typographie‹ war der Titel eines

9 Punkt auf 4 mm
9 points on 4 mm

»Neue Typographie« als Schlagwort und
als Titel hatte zur Zeit des Erscheinens von
Tschicholds Buch schon Geschichte. ›Die
Neue Typographie‹ war der Titel eines

9 Punkt auf 4,5 mm
9 points on 4,5 mm

»Neue Typographie« als Schlagwort und
als Titel hatte zur Zeit des Erscheinens von
Tschicholds Buch schon Geschichte. ›Die
Neue Typographie‹ war der Titel eines

9 Punkt auf 3,5 mm
9 points on 3,5 mm

»Neue Typographie« als Schlagwort und als Titel hatte zur Zeit des
Erscheinens von Tschicholds Buch schon Geschichte. ›Die Neue
Typographie‹ war der Titel eines programmatischen Aufsatzes von
Laszlo Moholy-Nagy im ›Bauhausbuch‹ 1923, das im Zusammen-

9 Punkt auf 3,75 mm
9 points on 3,75 mm

»Neue Typographie« als Schlagwort und als Titel hatte zur Zeit des
Erscheinens von Tschicholds Buch schon Geschichte. ›Die Neue
Typographie‹ war der Titel eines programmatischen Aufsatzes von
Laszlo Moholy-Nagy im ›Bauhausbuch‹ 1923, das im Zusammen-

	44	68	92
Buchstaben Characters	44	68	92
Zeilenlänge (mm) Length of lines (mm)	67,5	105	142,5

9 Punkt auf 4 mm
9 points on 4 mm

Editors, printers, designers, ophthalmologists, and educators have been concerned with the legibility of print for more than a century. In the earlier years, there were many opinions and recommendations expressed on this subject; however, these were based on casual obser-

9 Punkt auf 4,5 mm
9 points on 4,5 mm

Editors, printers, designers, ophthalmologists, and educators have been concerned with the legibility of print for more than a century. In the earlier years, there were many opinions and recommendations expressed on this subject; however, these were based on casual obser-

9 Punkt auf 3,5 mm
9 points on 3,5 mm

Editors, printers, designers, ophthalmologists, and educators have been concerned with the legibility of print for more than a century. In the earlier years, there were many opinions and recommendations expressed on this subject; however, these were based on casual observation rather than upon research findings. Prior to 1900, there were very few experimental studies

9 Punkt auf 3,75 mm
9 points on 3,75 mm

Editors, printers, designers, ophthalmologists, and educators have been concerned with the legibility of print for more than a century. In the earlier years, there were many opinions and recommendations expressed on this subject; however, these were based on casual observation rather than upon research findings. Prior to 1900, there were very few experimental studies

9 Punkt auf 4 mm
9 points on 4 mm

Editors, printers, designers, ophthalmologists, and educators have been concerned with the legibility of print for more than a century. In the earlier years, there were many opinions and recommendations expressed on this subject; however, these were based on casual observation rather than upon research findings. Prior to 1900, there were very few experimental studies

9 Punkt auf 4,5 mm
9 points on 4,5 mm

Editors, printers, designers, ophthalmologists, and educators have been concerned with the legibility of print for more than a century. In the earlier years, there were many opinions and recommendations expressed on this subject; however, these were based on casual observation rather than upon research findings. Prior to 1900, there were very few experimental studies

Das sichtbare Linienbild (Linienstärke) wird je nach Satzsystem (Bleisatz oder Fotosatz) in Punkten oder Millimetern gemessen. Im Bleisatz kommen vorfabrizierte Einheitsmessinglinien (4 Punkt bis 24 Cicero/Pica) und individuell bestimmbare Bleilinien (bis etwa 80 cm Länge) zur Anwendung. Im Fotosatz kann jede gewünschte Stärke und Länge belichtet werden. Dem Gestalter genügen jedoch die vom Hersteller definierten Stärken. In beiden Systemen sind auch punktierte Linien und Schmucklinien erhältlich.

The visible image of the rule, or the rule weight, is measured in points or millimeters, depending on the typesetting system (metal or photosetting). For metal setting, standard lengths of brass rule (4 points to 24 cicero/picas) and individually cut type-metal rules up to approximately 30 inches in length are used. In photosetting, any desired weight and length of rule may be exposed, but the weights specified by the manufacturer should suffice for the designer's needs. Dotted and decorative rules are also obtainable.

mm-Linien (Berthold Fotosatz)

American points lines

0,075	Hairline
0,1	
0,15	½ point
0,25	
0,3125	1 point
0,375	
0,5	1½ points
0,75	
1,0	2 points
1,5	
	3 points
1,875	
2,0	4 points
2,25	
	6 points
2,5	
3,0	8 points
3,2	
	10 points
3,5	
4,0	12 points
4,25	
	18 points

Neben den Buchstaben, Ziffern und Linien steht eine unübersehbare Menge an Zeichen und Symbolen für die verschiedenen Sachgebiete zur Verfügung. Für spezielle Aufgaben hat der Gestalter die entsprechende Fachliteratur beizuziehen. Im Bleisatz ist das Angebot an Zeichen beschränkt. Der Fotosatz jedoch kennt keine Grenzen, denn Zeichen und Symbole können jeder Schriftgrösse angepasst werden.

In addition to letters, numbers and rules, a great many signs and symbols are available for various fields of typesetting. For special jobs, the designer should refer to the appropriate specimen sheets. Whereas the range of special sorts for metal setting is limited, photosetting has infinite possibilities in this sector and allows signs and symbols to be produced in any required size.

Nicht alle typografischen Arbeiten verlangen einen typografischen Raster. Ein Einzelblatt, ein einmaliges Typoplakat, ein Typozeichen oder eine Typoskulptur sind durchaus ohne Raster zu entwickeln. Im gesamten typografischen Geschehen sind dies aber eher Einzelfälle.

Die Mehrheit der typografischen Aufgaben ist umfangreich und sehr komplex; ein Buch zum Beispiel besteht aus vielen Druckseiten mit Informationen verschiedenster Art, ist ein- oder mehrsprachig, enthält nur Text oder Text und Bild. Oder eine Information wird als Serie publiziert, eine Serie von Plakaten, eine Serie von Inseraten usw. Dasselbe gilt auch für den Bildschirm.

Um derartige Aufgaben unter Kontrolle zu halten und auch wirtschaftlich zu realisieren, benötigt der Gestalter eine logische, konstante Grundlage mit mehr oder weniger Variablen. Ein typografischer Raster, ein typografisches System ist wie ein Spielfeld. Ein solches schränkt die Kreativität des Spielers nicht ein, aber es ordnet und setzt Grenzen. (Es gibt gute und schlechte Schachspieler, die Einteilung des Feldes ist für alle gleich.) Der Gestalter ist bei der Wahl seines Spielfeldes freier, er bestimmt die Einteilung weitgehend selbst. Er bestimmt, entsprechend der zu lösenden Aufgabe, wie einfach oder eben differenziert er seinen typografischen Raster entwickelt.

Der typografische Raster regelt aber nicht nur die Schriftanordnungen auf einer Seite, sondern ebenso die Anordnung der Bilder (Umbruch von Text und Bild).

Not all typographical jobs require a typographical grid. A single sheet, a one-off typographical poster, a single sign or a typographical ''picture'' may be produced without the use of any kind of grid, but these are by way of being exceptions in the field of typography as a whole.

Most typographical jobs are voluminous and complex. A book, for example, consists of many pages containing the most varied kind of information; it may be in one or more languages and may contain text only or a mixture of text and graphics. Information may be published in serial form as well: as a series of posters, advertisements, etc. The same applies to the visual display screen.

In order to keep such productions under control and to operate economically, the designer needs a logical and constant basis with a greater or lesser number of variables. A typographical grid or system is like a playing field, which does not limit the player's creativity but orders the game and sets boundaries. The chessboard, after all, is the same for both good and bad players. The designer is freer in the choice of his field of play, to a great extent setting up its divisions himself. In accordance with the nature of the job in hand, he determines the simplicity or the differentiation of the development of his typographical grid.

The typographical grid governs not only the arrangement of type on a page but also that of the pictures in the make-up of text and graphics.

Der Aufbau eines typografischen Rasters

Eine Fläche, zum Beispiel das Papierformat, wird eingeteilt in die zu bedruckende Fläche und die nicht zu bedruckende Fläche. Die zu bedruckende Fläche nennen wir Satzspiegel. Die nicht zu bedruckenden Flächen sind die Aussenflächen (siehe Seite 61).

Der typografische Raster bestimmt die Masse des Satzspiegels, dessen Einteilung und die Aussenflächen. Die Masse des typografischen Rasters müssen den Massen der typografischen Elemente entsprechen (Punkt/mm). Die Einteilung der typografischen Fläche ist in der Regel vertikal und horizontal.

Construction of a Typographical Grid

An area, i.e. the sheet or page size, is divided into the area to be printed and the area not to be printed. We call the area to be printed the type area. The areas not to be printed are the outer areas or margins (see page 61).

The typographical grid determines the dimensions of the type area, its divisions and its margins. The grid must be measured in the typographical units in use: points, inches or millimeters. The divisions are usually vertical and horizontal.

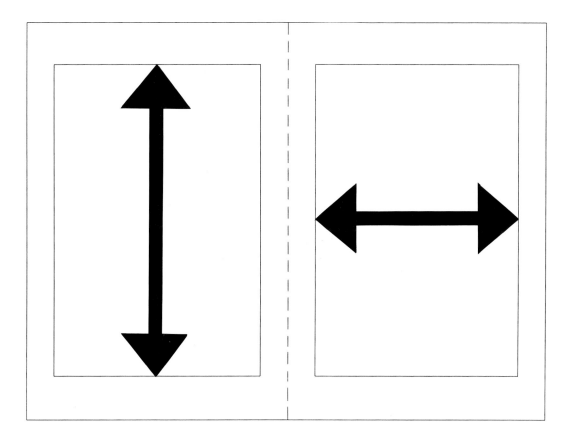

Die vertikale Einteilung des Satzspiegels

Die vertikale Einteilung entspricht immer dem Mass einer Zeile, das heisst dem Mass von Zeile zu Zeile des Haupttextes (Mengensatz).

Die vom Gestalter festgelegte Anzahl von Zeilen ergibt die konstante Höhe des Satzspiegels.

Beispiel mit 12 Punkt von Zeile zu Zeile:

Haupttext	12 Punkt kompress oder 10 Punkt mit 2 Punkt Durchschuss
Legenden	6 Punkt kompress
Titel	24, 36, 48 und 60 Punkt

Alle diese Grössen entsprechen genau der vertikalen Teilung in 12 Punkt.

Beispiel mit 3 mm von Zeile zu Zeile:

Haupttext	8 Punkt auf 3 mm
Legenden	6 Punkt auf 2,25 mm
Titel	16 Punkt auf 6 mm
	24 Punkt auf 9 mm
	32 Punkt auf 12 mm

Bei diesem Beispiel entsprechen die Haupttexte und die Titel der vertikalen Teilung in 3 mm.

Die Legenden finden immer nach 4 Zeilen (4×2,25 mm = 9 mm) die Übereinstimmung mit 3 Haupttextzeilen (3×3 mm = 9 mm).

Vertical Division of Type Area

The vertical division is always measured in lines, i.e. using the distance from line to line of the main text (continuous setting) as the unit of measurement.

The number of lines per page specified by the designer gives a constant depth to the type area.

Example with 12 points from line to line:

Main text	12 points set solid or 10 points with 2 points leaded
Captions	6 points set solid
Headings	24, 36, 48, and 60 points

All these sizes exactly conform to the vertical division into units of 12 points.

Example with 3 mm from line to line:

Main text	8 points on 3 mm
Captions	6 points on 2.25 mm
Headings	16 points on 6 mm
	24 points on 9 mm
	32 points on 12 mm

In this example the main text and the headings conform to the vertical division into units of 3 mm.

Every 4 caption lines equal 3 text lines (4×2.25 = 9 mm, 3×3 = 9 mm).

Grundschriftgrösse 12 Punkt
kompress
Basic type size 12 points
set solid

Grundschriftgrösse 10 Punkt
mit 2 Punkt Durchschuss
Basic type size 10 points
with 2 points leaded

Legendenschriftgrösse 6 Punkt
kompress
Caption type size 6 points
set solid

Titel 24 Punkt

Title 36

Title 48

Titel 60

Grundschriftgrösse
8 Punkt / 3 mm
Basic type size
8 points / 3 mm

Legendengrösse
6 Punkt / 2,25 mm
Caption type size
6 points / 2.25 mm

Titel 16 Punkt

Title 24 points

Titel 32 Punkt

Die horizontale Einteilung des Satzspiegels

Horizontal Division of Type Area

Die horizontale Einteilung des Satzspiegels bestimmt die Anzahl und Breite der Spalten. Die Spalten sind jedoch weitgehend von der Grösse der Haupttexte abhängig, das heisst von der gewünschten Anzahl Buchstaben pro Zeile (siehe auch S. 42). Die Spaltenabstände haben eine eindeutige Trennung der Spalten zu gewährleisten.

In vielen Drucksachen finden wir Satzspiegel mit zwei, drei oder vier Spalten. Bücher sind vielfach einspaltig. Spezielle Imprimate auch 5-, 6- und 7spaltig.

Der Gestalter bestimmt die konstante Breite des Satzspiegels, welche seinen Bedürfnissen entsprechend in Spalten teilbar ist.

The horizontal division of the type area determines the number and width of the columns. However, their width largely depends on the size of the text typeface, i.e. on the desired number of characters per line (see also p.42). The distances between columns must ensure that they are clearly separated from one another.

Many kinds of printed matter have type areas divided into two, three or four columns. Books are usually single-column but some publications may have 5, 6 or 7 columns to the page.

The designer specifies the constant width of the type area, which is divisible into columns in accordance with his needs.

Horizontale Einteilung des Satzspiegels für dieses Buch: 3,75 mm, 5 Spalten zu 30 mm, 7,5 mm Spaltenabstand

Horizontal division of type area for this book: 3.75 mm, five 30-mm columns, 7.5 mm from column to column

| 30 | 7,5 | 30 | 7,5 | 30 | 7,5 | 30 | 7,5 | 30 |

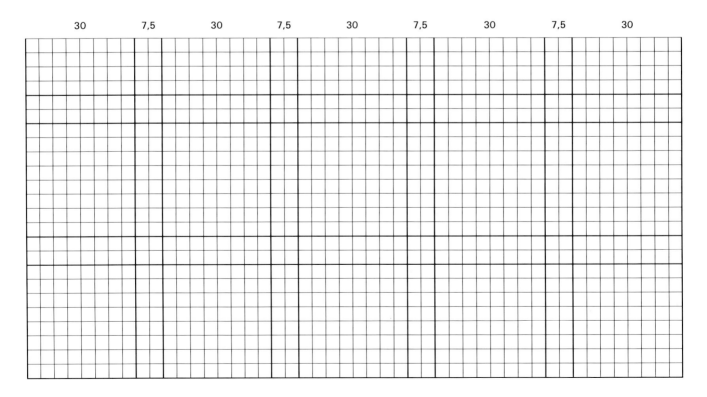

Der Rasteraufbau mit Einheiten

Sind wir an einem möglichst variablen typografischen Raster interessiert, so beginnen wir unsere Überlegungen zuerst in Einheiten, wobei wir die vertikale Einheit als einen Zeilenabstand (für Haupttexte) verstehen.

Diese vertikale Einheit kann auch horizontal verwendet werden. Somit arbeiten wir mit einem Quadrat als Baustein, zum Beispiel 10×10 Punkt oder 4×4 mm (andere Proportionen sind denkbar, doch sehr bald für die Praxis zu kompliziert).

Damit nun unser Raster so variabel wie möglich wird, das heisst variabel für Text und Bild, suchen wir auf die ganze Breite und die ganze Höhe des Satzspiegels diejenige Anzahl von Einheiten, die sich immer ohne Rest in verschiedene Teile (Spalten) bei immer gleichbleibenden Abständen (Spaltenabstände) teilen lässt.

Beispiele: 58 Einheiten sind bei immer 2 Einheiten als Abstand wie folgt teilbar:

in 2 Spalten $(2×28)+2$ $= 58$
in 3 Spalten $(3×18)+(2×2)$ $= 58$
in 4 Spalten $(4×13)+(3×2)$ $= 58$
in 5 Spalten $(5×10)+(4×2)$ $= 58$
in 6 Spalten $(6×8)+(5×2)$ $= 58$

59 Einheiten mit nur einer Einheit als Abstand sind wiederum in 2, 3, 4, 5 und 6 Spalten teilbar.

70 und 94 Einheiten mit immer 2 Einheiten als Abstand sind in 2, 3, 4, 6 und 8 Spalten teilbar.

Andere Reihen zu finden und die Umsetzung in Punkt oder Millimeter, ist nur eine Frage der Geduld, der Erfahrung und auch der Experimentierfreudigkeit.

Grid Construction in Units

If we are interested in obtaining a typographical grid with the greatest number of possible variations, we begin our plans with units, taking the vertical unit as space from line to line for.

This vertical unit may also be used horizontally, so that we work with a square as the building-block, e.g. 10×10 points or 4×4 mm. Other proportions are also possible but quickly become too complicated for practical use.

In order to make our grid as variable as possible for both text and graphics, we now look for a number of units across the width and from head to foot of the type area which can be divided into different parts (columns) with a constant amount of space between them, without leaving a remainder.

Examples: 58 units with a constant space of 2 units between columns may be divided as follows:

into 2 columns $(2×28) + 2$ $= 58$
into 3 columns $(3×18) + (2×2)$ $= 58$
into 4 columns $(4×13) + (3×2)$ $= 58$
into 5 columns $(5×10) + (4×2)$ $= 58$
into 6 columns $(6× 8) + (5×2)$ $= 58$

59 units with only one unit as space between columns can also be divided into 2, 3, 4, 5 and 6 columns.

70 and 94 units with always 2 units as space can be divided into 2, 3, 4, 6, and 8 columns.

Finding other series and the conversion into points, inches or millimeters is only a matter of patience, experience and willingness to experiment.

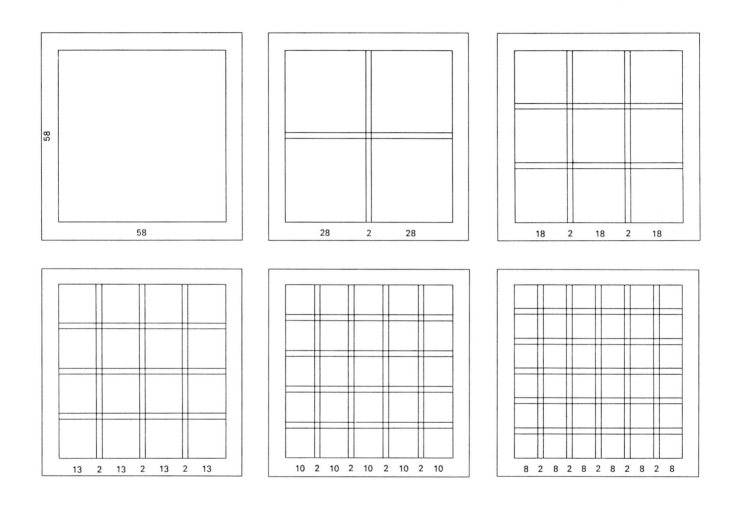

58

58

28 2 28

18 2 18 2 18

13 2 13 2 13 2 13

10 2 10 2 10 2 10 2 10

8 2 8 2 8 2 8 2 8 2 8

Quadratraster mit
58 Einheiten.
Spaltenabstand
2 Einheiten.
Vertikal und horizontal
gleiche Grösse der
Einheiten

Square grid with
58 units.
Distance between
columns 2 units.
Vertical and horizontal
units of same size.

Beispiel 58

Neue Typographie als Schlagwort und als Titel hatte zur Zeit des Erscheinens von Tschicholds Buch schon Geschichte. ›Die Neue Typographie‹ war der Titel eines programmatischen Aufsatzes von Laszlo Moholy-Nagy im ›Bauhausbuch‹ 1923, das im Zusammenhang mit der ›Bauhaus-Ausstellung‹ in Weimar erschienen ist, die auch Jan Tschichold umgekehrt hat. Moholy-Nagy fordert darin »zuallererst: eindeutige Klarheit in allen typographischen Werken. Die Lesbarkeit – die Mitteilung darf nie unter einer a priori angenommenen Aesthetik leiden. Die Buchstabentypen dürfen nie in eine vorbestimmte Form, z.B. ein Quadrat gezwängt werden.« Ein Jahr später, 1924, Schreibt Moholy-Nagy seinen Aufsatz ›Zeitgemäße Typographie. Ziele, Praxis, Kritik und 1926 neben Aufsätzen zur Schriftform von Josef Albers und Herbert Bayer im Bauhaus-Sonderheft der Zeitschrift ›Offset‹. Schlagworte und Forderungen sind »Ausnutzung maschineller Möglichkeiten«, »Klarheit, Knappheit, Präzision«, »Einheitsschrift, ohne Minuskeln und Majuskeln; nur Einheitsbuchstaben – nicht der Größe, sondern der Form nach.« Herbert Bayer läßt später auf die Briefblätter des ›bauhaus dessau‹ in die Impressumszeile drucken: »wir schreiben alles klein, denn wir sparen damit zeit. Drei Monate nach der ›Offset‹-Nummer erscheint das Sonderheft ›elementare typographie‹ der ›Typographischen Mitteilungen‹, der Zeitschrift der Setzer und Drucker, herausgegeben von Iwan Tschichold, »Typographie des Heftes: Ivan Tschichold, Leipzig«. Sein einleitender Aufsatz ›Die Neue Gestaltung‹ nimmt die Methode des Buches ›Die Neue Typographie‹ vorweg. Tschichold referiert die Entwicklung der Avantgarde, insbesondere der Malerei der letzten Jahrzehnte und versucht, die neue Typographie als Ergebnis der konsequenten Arbeit des russischen Suprematismus, des holländischen Neoplastizismus (De Stijl, G.F.) und insbesondere des Konstruktivismus darzustellen. »Neue Typographie‹ als Schlagwort und als Titel hatte zur Zeit des Erscheinens von Tschicholds Buch schon Geschichte. ›Die Neue Typographie‹ war der Titel eines

58

Neue Typographie als Schlagwort und als Titel

hatte zur Zeit des Erscheinens von Tschicholds Buch schon Geschichte. ›Die Neue Typographie‹ war der Titel eines programmatischen Aufsatzes von Laszlo Moholy-Nagy im ›Bauhausbuch‹ 1923, das im Zusammenhang mit der ›Bauhaus-Ausstellung‹ in Weimar erschienen ist, die auch Jan Tschichold umgekehrt hat. Moholy-Nagy fordert darin »zuallererst: eindeutige Klarheit in allen typographischen Werken. Die Lesbarkeit – die Mitteilung darf nie

Ein Jahr später, 1924, schreibt Moholy-Nagy seinen Aufsatz ›Zeitgemäße

Typographie. Ziele, Praxis, Kritik und 1926 neben Aufsätzen zur Schriftform von Josef Albers und Herbert Bayer im Bauhaus-Sonderheft der Zeitschrift ›Offset‹. Schlagworte und Forderungen sind »Ausnutzung maschineller Möglichkeiten«, »Klarheit, Knappheit, Präzision«, »Einheitsschrift, ohne Minuskeln und Majuskeln; nur Einheitsbuchstaben – nicht der Größe, sondern der Form nach.« Herbert Bayer läßt später auf die Briefblätter des ›bauhaus dessau‹ in der Impressumszeile drucken:

28 2 28

Neue Typographie als Schlagwort

und als Titel hatte zur Zeit des Erscheinens von Tschicholds Buch schon Geschichte. ›Die Neue Typographie‹ war der Titel eines programmatischen Aufsatzes von Laszlo Moholy-Nagy im ›Bauhausbuch‹ 1923, das im Zusammenhang mit der ›Bauhaus-Ausstellung‹ in Weimar erschienen ist, die auch Jan Tschichold umge-

Ein Jahr später, 1924, schreibt Moholy-Nagy seinen

Aufsatz ›Zeitgemäße Typographie. Ziele, Praxis, Kritik und 1926 neben Aufsätzen zur Schriftform von Josef Albers und Herbert Bayer im Bauhaus-Sonderheft der Zeitschrift ›Offset‹. Schlagworte und Forderungen sind »Ausnutzung maschineller Möglichkeiten«,

Drei Monate nach der ›Offset‹-Nummer

erscheint das Sonderheft ›elementare typographie‹ der ›Typographischen Mitteilungen‹, der Zeitschrift der Setzer und Drucker, herausgegeben von Iwan Tschichold, »Typographie des Heftes: Ivan Tschichold, Leipzig«. Sein einleitender Aufsatz ›Die Neue Gestaltung‹ nimmt die Methode des Buches ›Die Neue Typographie‹ vorweg. Tschichold referiert die Entwicklung der Avantgarde, insbesondere der Malerei der letzten

18 2 18 2 18

Neue Typographie als Schlagwort und als Titel hatte zur Zeit

des Erscheinens von Tschicholds Buch schon Geschichte. ›Die Neue Typographie‹ war der Titel eines programmatischen Aufsatzes von Laszlo Moholy-Nagy im ›Bauhausbuch‹ 1923, das im Zusammenhang mit der ›Bauhaus-Ausstellung‹ in Weimar erschienen ist, die auch Jan Tschichold umgekehrt hat. Moholy-Nagy fordert darin »zuallererst: eindeutige Klarheit in allen typographischen Werken. Die Lesbarkeit – die Mitteilung darf nie unter

einer a priori angenommenen Aesthetik leiden. Die Buchstabentypen dürfen nie in eine vorbestimmte Form, z.B. ein Quadrat gezwängt werden.« Ein Jahr später, 1924, Schreibt Moholy-Nagy seinen Aufsatz ›Zeitgemäße Typographie. Ziele, Praxis, Kritik und 1926 neben Aufsätzen zur Schriftform von Josef Albers und Herbert Bayer im Bauhaus-Sonderheft der Zeitschrift ›Offset‹. Schlagworte und Forderungen sind »Ausnutzung maschineller

Möglichkeiten«, »Klarheit, Knappheit, Präzision«, »Einheitsschrift, ohne Minuskeln und Majuskeln; nur Einheitsbuchstaben – nicht der Form nach.« Herbert Bayer läßt später auf die Briefblätter des ›bauhaus dessau‹ in der Impressumszeile drucken: »wir schreiben alles klein, denn wir sparen damit zeit.« Drei Monate nach der ›Offset‹-Nummer erscheint das Sonderheft ›elementare typographie‹ der ›Typographischen

13 2 13 2 13 2 13

Neue Typographie als Schlagwort und als Titel

Ein Jahr später, 1924, Schreibt Moholy-Nagy seinen Aufsatz ›Zeitgemäße Typographie. Ziele, Praxis, Kritik und 1926 neben

Schlagworte und Forderungen sind »Ausnutzung maschineller Möglichkeiten«

Drei Monate nach der ›Offset‹-Nummer erscheint das Sonderheft ›elementare typographie‹ der ›Typographischen Mitteilungen‹, der Zeitschrift der Setzer

hatte zur Zeit des Erscheinens von Tschicholds Buch schon Geschichte. ›Die Neue Typographie‹ war der Titel eines programmatischen Aufsatzes von Laszlo Moholy-Nagy im ›Bauhausbuch‹ 1923, das im Zusammenhang mit der ›Bauhaus-Ausstellung‹ in Weimar erschienen ist, die auch Jan Tschichold umgekehrt hat. Moholy-Nagy fordert darin »zuallererst: eindeutige Klarheit in allen typographischen Werken. Die Lesbarkeit – die Mitteilung darf nie unter einer a priori angenommenen Aesthetik leiden. Die Buchstabentypen dürfen nie in eine vorbestimmte Form, z.B. ein Quadrat gezwängt werden.« Ein Jahr später,

1924, Schreibt Moholy-Nagy seinen Aufsatz ›Zeitgemäße Typographie. Ziele, Praxis, Kritik und 1926 neben Aufsätzen zur Schriftform von Josef Albers und Herbert Bayer im Bauhaus-Sonderheft der Zeitschrift ›Offset‹. Schlagworte und Forderungen sind »Ausnutzung maschineller Möglichkeiten«, »Klarheit, Knappheit, Präzision«, »Einheitsschrift, ohne Minuskeln und Majuskeln; nur Einheitsbuchstaben – nicht der Größe, sondern der Form nach.« Herbert Bayer läßt später auf die Briefblätter des ›bauhaus dessau‹ in der Impressumszeile drucken: »wir schreiben alles klein, denn wir sparen damit zeit.« Drei Monate

10 2 10 2 10 2 10 2 10

Neue Typographie als Schlagwort und

›Die Neue Typographie‹ war der Titel eines programmatischen Aufsatzes von Laszlo Moholy-

Moholy-Nagy fordert darin »zuallererst: eindeutige Klarheit in allen typographi-

als Titel hatte zur Zeit des Erscheinens von Tschicholds Buch schon Geschichte. ›Die Neue Typographie‹ war der Titel eines programmatischen Aufsatzes von Laszlo Moholy-Nagy im ›Bauhausbuch‹ 1923, das im Zusammenhang mit der ›Bauhaus-Ausstellung‹ in Weimar erschienen ist, die auch Jan Tschichold umgekehrt hat. Moholy-Nagy fordert darin »zuallererst: eindeutige Klarheit in allen typographischen Werken. Die Lesbarkeit – die Mitteilung darf nie unter einer a priori angenommenen Aesthetik leiden. Die Buchstaben-

typen dürfen nie in eine vorbestimmte Form, z.B. ein Quadrat gezwängt werden.« Ein Jahr später, 1924, schreibt Moholy-Nagy seinen Aufsatz ›Zeitgemäße Typographie. Ziele, Praxis, Kritik und 1926 neben Aufsätzen zur Schriftform von Josef Albers und Herbert Bayer im Bauhaus-Sonderheft der Zeitschrift ›Offset‹. Schlagworte und Forderungen sind »Ausnutzung maschineller Möglichkeiten«, »Klarheit, Knappheit, Präzision«, »Einheitsschrift, ohne Minuskeln und Majuskeln; nur Einheitsbuchstaben – nicht

Die Lesbarkeit – die Mitteilung darf nie unter einer

Die Buchstaben typen dürfen nie in eine vorbestimmte Form, z.B. ein Quadrat gezwängt werden.

Ein Jahr später, 1924, Schreibt Moholy-Nagy

8 2 8 2 8 2 8 2 8

Umbruchbeispiele
Layout examples

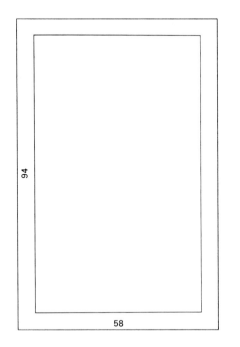

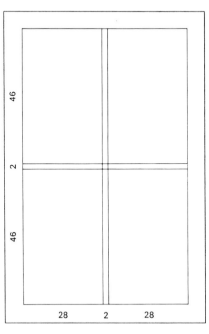

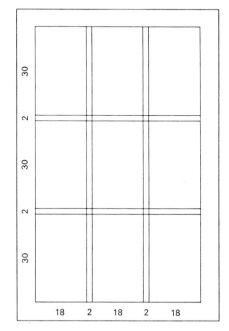

Rechteckraster,
vertikal 94 Einheiten,
horizontal 58 Einheiten.
Vertikal und horizontal
gleiche Grösse der
Einheiten.

Rectangular grid,
vertical 94 units,
horizontal 58 units.
Vertical and horizontal
units of same size.

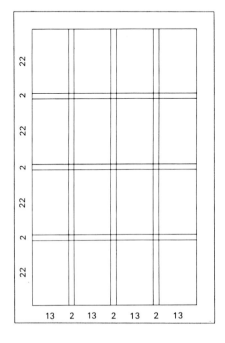

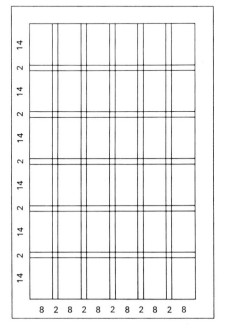

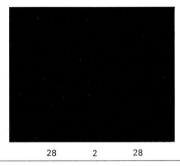

94

58

Editors, printers, ophthalmologists

and educators have been concerned with the legibility of print for more than a century. In the earlier years, there were many opinions and recommendations expressed on this subject; however, these were based on casual observation rather than upon research findings. Prior to 1900, there were very few experimental studies reported, but since 1925, research in the field has expanded markedly. Before the nineteenth century, the main concern was with esthetic appearance of print. With improved technology

of printing, two additional factors entered the picture: Economy of printing and traditional practices. For many years, these three factors dominated the arrangement of the printed page. These emphases are still operating, although to a somewhat lesser degree. Because of these practices and views, a truly scientific typography has been slow in developing. This discussion of legibility of print is concerned primarily with printed material to be read by adults. At what level do children read enough like adults so that is

28 2 28

Editors, printers, designers, ophthalmologists, and educators

have been concerned with the legibility of print

markedly. Before the nineteenth century, the main concern was with esthetic appearance of print. With improved technology of printing, two additional factors entered the picture: Economy of printing

for more than a century. In the earlier years, there were many opinions and recommendations expressed on this subject; however, these were based on casual observation rather than upon research findings. Prior to 1900, there were very few experimental studies reported, but since 1925, research in the field has expanded marked-

and traditional practices. For many

years, these three factors dominated the arrangement of the printed page. These emphases are still operating, although to a somewhat lesser degree. Because of these practices and views, a truly scientific typography has been slow in developing. This discussion of legibility of print is concerned primarily with printed material to be read by adults. At what level do children read enough like adults so that it is not necessary to differentiate between the two in a discussion of the legibility of print? The results of two investigations provide an answer to this question. In a study of eye movements of children during reading, Buswell found a definite stabilization of the oculomotor patterns by the end of the 4th grade. In the

18 2 18 2 18

Editors, printers, designers, ophthalmologists, and educators have been concerned with the legibility of print for more than a century. In the earlier years, there were many opinions and recommendations expressed on this subject; however, these were based on casual observation rather than upon research findings. Prior to 1900, there were very few experimental studies reported, but since 1925, re-

search in the field has expanded markedly. Before the nineteenth century, the main concern was with esthetic appearance of print. With improved technology of printing, two additional factors entered the picture: Economy of printing and traditional practices. For many years, these three factors dominated the arrangement of the printed page. These emphases are still operating,

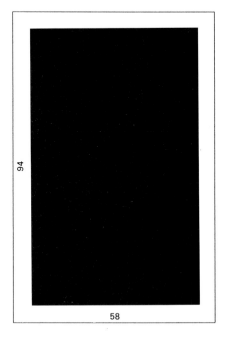

emphases are still operating, although to a somewhat lesser degree. Because of these practices and views, a truly scientific typography has been slow in developing. This discussion of legibility of print is concerned primarily with printed material to be read by adults. At what

level do children read enough like adults so that it is not necessary to differentiate between the two in a discussion of the legibility of print? The results of two investigations provide an answer to this question. In a study of eye movements of children during reading, Buswell found a definite stabilization of the oculomotor patterns by the end of the 4th grade. In the second investigation, Ballantine discovered rapid gains in eye-movement

the 4th and the 8th grades, i.e., between the ages of 10 and 13 years. This suggests that children read enough like

adults so typographical arrangements having optimal legibility for adults should also be optimal for children who are about 10 years of age or older. This is supported by some unpublished data of the writer. Editors, printers, designers, ophthalmologists, and educators have been concerned with the legibility of print for more than a century. In the earlier years, there were many opinions and recommendations expressed on this subject; however, these were based on casual observation rather than upon research findings. Prior to 1900, there were very few experimental studies reported, but since 1925, research in the field has

efficiency from the 2nd to the 4th grade and slower progress from the 4th to the 8th grade. Since oculomotor behavior represents efficiency in the mechanics of reading, one may conclude from these studies that the mechanics of reading becomes well stabilized, or like that of adults, somewhere between

13 2 13 2 13 2 13

Editors, printers, designers, ophthalmologists, and educators

have been concerned with the legibility of print for more than a century. In the earlier years, there were many opinions and recommendations expressed on this subject; however, these were based on casual observation rather than upon research findings. Prior to 1900, there were very few experimental studies reported, but since 1925, research in the field has expanded markedly. Before the nineteenth century, the

main concern was with esthetic appearance of print. With improved technology of printing, two additional factors entered the picture: Economy of printing and traditional practices. For many years, these three factors dominated the arrangement of the printed page. These emphases are still operating, although to a somewhat lesser degree. Because of these practices and views, a truly scientific typography has been

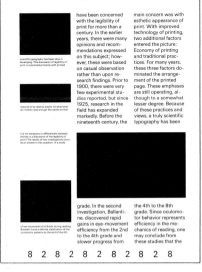

scientific typography has been slow in developing. This discussion of legibility of print is concerned primarily with printed

material to be read by adults. At what level do children read enough like adults so that

it is not necessary to differentiate between the two in a discussion of the legibility of print? The results of two investigations provide an answer to this question. In a study

of eye movements of children during reading, Buswell found a definite stabilization of the oculomotor patterns by the end of the 4th

grade. In the second investigation, Ballantine discovered rapid gains in eye-movement efficiency from the 2nd to the 4th grade and slower progress from

the 4th to the 8th grade. Since oculomotor behavior represents efficiency in the mechanics of reading, one may conclude from these studies that the

8 2 8 2 8 2 8 2 8 2 8

Umbruchbeispiele
Layout examples

Übereinstimmung von Schrift und Bild im Raster

Unser Raster basiert auf einer gleichmässigen Teilung des Satzspiegels.

Damit nun Bild und Text in jedem Fall auf gleicher Höhe beginnen, haben wir beide auf gleicher Höhe zu plazieren, die obere Bildkante genau auf die Rasterlinie, die Kopflinie der Schrift ebenso. Die Bildhöhe messen wir von Rasterlinie zu Rasterlinie (bei einem 3,75-mm-Raster zum Beispiel 30 mm). Diese 30 mm entsprechen 8 Zeilen einer 9-Punkt-Schrift auf 3,75 mm Zeilenabstand gesetzt. Die Differenz zwischen Bildhöhe und Schriftbild, das heisst der sichtbare Zeilenzwischenraum, erscheint nun gegenüber der unteren Bildkante. Doch unten wird dies kaum beachtet.

Diese vielleicht etwas ungewohnte Art der Rasteranwendung bringt jedoch den grossen Vorteil eines einheitlichen Masssystems für Text und Bild.

Coordination of Type and Graphics in the Grid

Our grid is based on a uniform division of the type area.

In order to ensure that picture and text always start at the same level, we must mount them both at the same height, placing both the upper edge of the picture and the cap line of the type on the same grid line. We measure the depth of the picture in numbers of grid lines, e.g. 30 mm with a 3.75-mm grid, the 30 mm equalling 8 lines of a 9-point type set on a 3.75-mm body. The difference between the depth of the picture and the type image, that is the visible line spacing, now appears against the lower edge of the picture, where it is scarcely noticeable.

This way of using a grid, although perhaps rather unusual, has the advantage of providing a uniform system of measurement for both text and pictures.

3,75-mm-Raster:
3,75-mm grid:

7 Punkt / 3 mm
(5 × 3 mm = 15 mm,
4 × 3,75 mm = 15 mm)

9 Punkt / 3,75 mm

18 Punkt / 7,5 mm

Schrift und Bild
im Raster

Unser Raster basiert auf einer gleichmässigen Teilung des Satzspiegels.

Damit nun Bild und Text in jedem Fall auf
gleicher Höhe beginnen, haben wir beide auf
gleicher Höhe zu plazieren, die obere Bildkante genau auf die Rasterlinie, die Kopflinie
der Schrift ebenso. Die Bildhöhe messen wir
von Rasterlinie zu Rasterlinie (bei einem
3,75-mm-Raster zum Beispiel 30 mm). Diese
30 mm entsprechen 8 Zeilen einer 9-Punkt-
Schrift auf 3,75 mm Zeilenabstand gesetzt.
Die Differenz zwischen Bildhöhe und Schriftbild, das heisst der sichtbare Zeilenzwischenraum, erscheint nun gegenüber der unteren
Bildkante. Doch unten wird dies kaum
beachtet.

Diese vielleicht etwas ungewohnte Art der
Rasteranwendung bringt jedoch den grossen
Vorteil eines einheitlichen Masssystems für
Text und Bild.

Our grid is based on a uniform division of the
type area.
In order to ensure that picture and text always start at the same level, we must mount
them both at the same height, placing both
the upper edge of the picture and the cap
line of the type on the same grid line. We
measure the depth of the picture in numbers
of grid lines, e.g. 30 mm with a 3,75-mm grid,
the 30 mm equalling 8 lines of a 9-point type
set on a 3,75-mm body. The difference
between the depth of the picture and the
type image, that is the visible line spacing,
now appears against the lower edge of
the picture, where it is scarcely noticeable.
This way of using a grid, although perhaps
rather unusual, has the advantage of providing a uniform system of measurement for

3,75-mm-Raster:
3,75-mm grid:
7 Punkt / 3 mm
(5 × 3 mm = 15 mm,
4 × 3,75 mm = 15 mm)
9 Punkt / 3,75 mm
18 Punkt / 7,5 mm

7,5 mm

30 mm

30 mm   7,5 mm

Die Aussenflächen

Die Aussenflächen umfassen den unbedruckten Teil einer Seite. Sie sind ein integrierter Bestandteil des Rasters und mit denselben Massen festzuhalten. Die Abstände vom Satzspiegel zu den vier Seiten des Formates sind der Art der Arbeit und der Einteilung des Satzspiegels entsprechend abzustimmen, gleichmässig oder verschieden.

Die Masse des Satzspiegels und die einmal festgelegten Randabstände bleiben konstant.

Bei einer mehrseitigen Arbeit, wenn nur schon Vor- und Rückseite eines Blattes bedruckt werden, ist zu entscheiden, ob sich ' der Satzspiegel in der Durchsicht deckt oder nicht (Register).

Für mehrseitige Drucksachen ist der Raster immer doppelseitig zu entwickeln. Soll der Satzspiegel der Vorderseite mit dem der Rückseite übereinstimmen, muss der Raster einer Doppelseite spiegelverkehrt angelegt werden. Diese Übereinstimmung der Satzspiegel ist vor allem bei dünnen, durchscheinenden Papierqualitäten wichtig. Verschiebungen des Satzspiegels verlangen dichte Papiersorten.

Die Randabstände rechts und links des Satzspiegels wählen wir grösser als den Abstand von Spalte zu Spalte. Der Randabstand im Bund ist zudem auf den Umfang und die Bindeart einer Drucksache abzustimmen.

Margins

The margins are the unprinted outer parts of a page. They form an integral part of the grid pattern and must be specified in the same units. The distances from the type area to the four edges of the page must be specified in accordance with the kind of work concerned and the division of the type area, and may be all equal or of different dimensions.

The dimensions of the type area and of the margins, once established, remain constant.

With a product of many pages, or even one page printed on both sides, a decision must be made as to whether the type areas on the two sides are to "back up" (register exactly).

For multi-page work, a double-spread grid must always be prepared.

Where the type area of the recto side must exactly cover that of the verso, the double-spread grid must be laid out in mirror fashion. This matching of type areas is particularly important for lightweight paper stocks with show-through characteristics. Conversely, specification of type areas which do not back each other up calls for the use of a heavier paper.

The left and right margin widths must be greater than the distances between columns.

Specification of the "gutter" margin must also take into account the thickness of the product and the method of binding to be used.

1
Aussenflächen
(nicht bedruckt)
Outer surfaces
(not printed)

2
Satzspiegel (bedruckt)
Type area (printed)

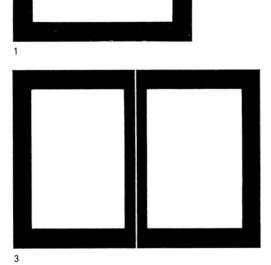

1

2

3
Registerhaltender
Satzspiegel
Type area matching
register

3

3

4
Verschobene Satzspiegel
Type area displaced

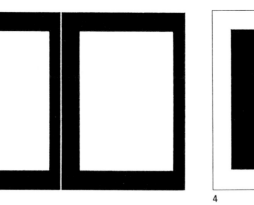

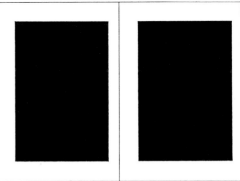

4

4

Kontraste   **Contrasts**

Kontraste entstehen durch starke Gegensätze, durch auffallende Unterschiede. Eine grosse Schrift ist nur gross im Vergleich zur Umgebung, zum Beispiel zum Papierformat oder zu einer kleinen Schrift in unmittelbarer Nachbarschaft. Die Unterschiede liegen zwischen Maximum und Minimum.

Im Bereich der Typografie sind Kontraste als Gestaltungsmittel von grosser Bedeutung. Kontraste helfen Texte organisieren. Kontraste erleichtern das Lesen. Die Aussage eines bestimmten Textteiles kann durch harmonische Kontraste zum übrigen Text massgeblich unterstützt werden. Kontraste wirken als Signale. Kontraste stimulieren, motivieren, fallen auf. Das heisst natürlich überhaupt nicht, dass nur Kontraste typografische Lösungsansätze bieten. Nur muss der Gestalter alle Möglichkeiten kennen und wissen: Soll seine Arbeit bewegt oder ruhig, laut oder leise oder bewegt und leise wirken? Kontraste erlauben es dem Gestalter, mit der Schrift spielerisch und spontan umzugehen.

Contrasts come about through strong oppositions or striking differences. A large type size is large only in comparison with its surroundings, e.g. the page size or a small type size next to it. The differences are between ''maximum'' and ''minimum''.

In typography contrasts are very important as elements of design. They help the designer to organize texts and can make reading easier. The content of a given part of a text can be considerably emphasized through harmonious contrast with the rest of the text. Contrasts have a signalling effect: they stimulate, motivate and catch the eye. Of course this does not mean that contrasts are the only answers to typographical problems. It is simply that the designer must know and understand all the possible ways of giving his work a lively or a tranquil effect and making it loud or restrained in appearance. Contrasts also allow the designer to treat type spontaneously and playfully.

d**d**

_k**k**

_k_ k

E E

H _H_

anticonstitutionnel

nez
air
sol
gel
eau
feu
île
lac
pas
riz
jeu
vol
mot
uni

Kontraste:
dünn-dick, klein-gross,
weich-hart, dunkel-hell,
gerade-schräg, horizontal-
vertikal, wenig-viel,
geordnet-ungeordnet

Contrasts:
thin-thick, small-large,
soft-hard, dark-light,
straight-oblique, horizontal-
vertical, little-much,
in order-not in order

ooo

ooooooooooo
ooooooooooo
ooooooooooo
ooooooooooo
ooooooooooo
ooooooooooo
ooooooooooo

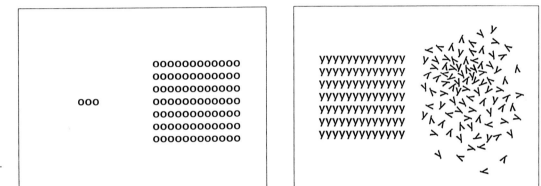

Proportionen nennen wir das Verhältnis verschiedener Grössen zueinander. Ein ausgewogen massvolles Verhältnis gilt als harmonisch. Harmonie erzeugt Genuss und Freude.

Proportionen finden wir in allen Dimensionen. Die Teilung von Linien, Flächen und Räumen ergibt immer bestimmte Verhältnisse der einzelnen Teile zueinander. Die einen sind langweilig, die andern spannungsvoll. Die einen sind regelmässig, die andern unregelmässig.

Beispiele von Teilungen einer Geraden in gleiche Teile mit verschiedenen Proportionen (Verhältnisse):

in 2 Teile, Verhältnis 1:1
in 3 Teile, Verhältnis 1:2
in 4 Teile, Verhältnis 1:3 und 2:2
in 5 Teile, Verhältnis 1:4, 2:3 (Pythagoras) und
    1:2:2
in 6 Teile, Verhältnis 1:5, 2:4, 3:3, 1:2:3
    und 2:2:2
in 7 Teile, Verhältnis 1:6, 2:5, 3:4, 1:2:4, 1:3:3,
    1:2:2:2
in 8 Teile, Verhältnis 1:7, 2:6, 3:5 (Goldener
    Schnitt), 4:4, 1:2:5 usw.

Alle diese Verhältnisse sind durchaus direkt für die gestalterische Arbeit mit Schrift verwendbar. Einerseits zur Bestimmung von Kontrasten der Schriftgrössen zueinander oder zur Bestimmung der Proportionen innerhalb eines typografischen Rasters (Satzspiegel, Spalten).

The relationship of size to size we call proportion.

A balanced relationship gives a harmonious effect, pleasing and satisfying to the eye.

Proportions exist in all dimensions. The arrangement of rules, solids and white space always produces certain proportions of part to part. Sometimes the effect is tedious, sometimes exciting; some relationships of dimension are regular, others irregular.

The following are some examples of divisions of a straight line into equal parts of different proportions (ratios):

into 2 parts, ratio   1:1
into 3 parts, ratio   1:2
into 4 parts, ratios   1:3 and 2:2
into 5 parts, ratios   1:4, 2:3 (Pythagoras)
                        and 1:2:2
into 6 parts, ratios   1:5, 2:4, 3:3, 1:2:3
                        and 2:2:2
into 7 parts, ratios   1:6, 2:5, 3:4, 1:2:4,
                        1:3:3, 1:2:2:2, etc.
into 8 parts, ratios   1:7, 2:6, 3:5 (golden
                        section), 4:4, 1:2:5, etc.

All these ratios are freely available for typographical design work, whether for the specification of contrasts between type sizes or of the proportions within a typographical grid, such as the type area and the arrangement into columns.

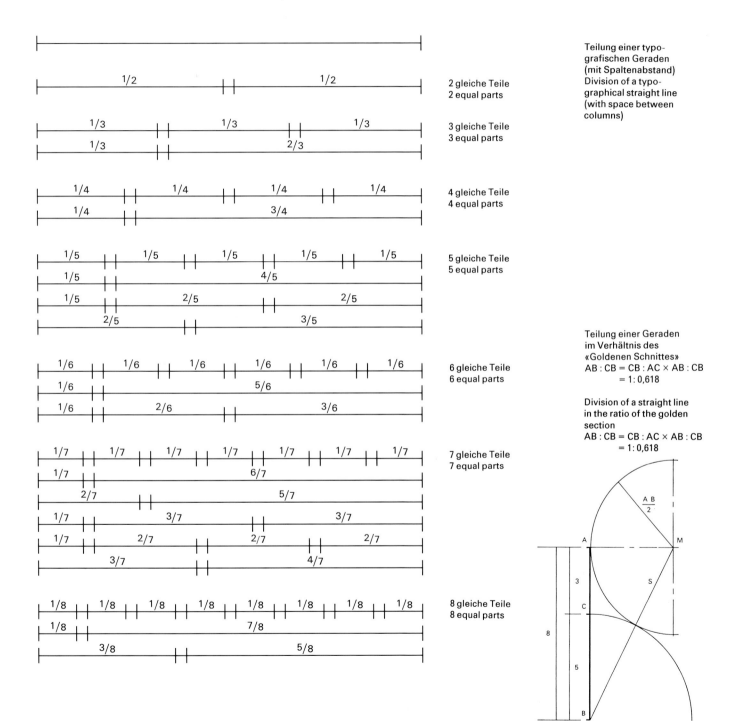

2 gleiche Teile
2 equal parts

3 gleiche Teile
3 equal parts

4 gleiche Teile
4 equal parts

5 gleiche Teile
5 equal parts

6 gleiche Teile
6 equal parts

7 gleiche Teile
7 equal parts

8 gleiche Teile
8 equal parts

Teilung einer typo-
grafischen Geraden
(mit Spaltenabstand)
Division of a typo-
graphical straight line
(with space between
columns)

Teilung einer Geraden
im Verhältnis des
«Goldenen Schnittes»
AB : CB = CB : AC × AB : CB
= 1 : 0,618

Division of a straight line
in the ratio of the golden
section
AB : CB = CB : AC × AB : CB
= 1 : 0,618

Als rhythmisch bezeichnen wir eine geregelte Bewegung oder einen regelmässigen, formbildenden Wechsel. Der Rhythmus einer typografischen Arbeit entsteht durch das gleichmässig gegliederte Wechselspiel von bedruckter zu unbedruckter Fläche, von Form zu Gegenform, von gross zu klein, von hell zu dunkel usw.

Die sich wiederholende typografische Sequenz, in einem Buch zum Beispiel der immer gleichbleibende Aufbau eines Kapitels oder auf einem typografischen Plakat die Betonung eines immer wiederkehrenden Buchstabens, dieser Rhythmus kann mit Zahlen festgehalten werden.

Beispiele von rhythmischen Zahlenreihen:

1212121212...
1414141414...
122112211221...
144114411441...
123123123123...
124124124124...
124812481248...
1248842112488421...
358358358358...
usw.

By rhythm we mean a controlled movement or a regular, form-producing interchange. The rhythm of a typographical work arises from the uniformly articulated counterplay of printed with unprinted areas, of form with counter-form, of large with small, light with dark, etc.

The repeated sequence in typography, for example the constant construction of chapters in a book or emphasis on a recurring character in a poster, forms a rhythm which can be defined in figures.

These are some examples of rhythmical sequences of figures:

1212121212...
1414141414...
122112211221...
144114411441...
123123123123...
124124124124...
124812481248...
1248842112488421...
358358358358...
etc.

TYPOGRAFIE

1 2 1 2 1 2 1 2

»Neue Typographie als Schlagwort und als Titel hatte zur Zeit des Erschei-

nens von Tschicholds Buch schon Geschichte.

›Die Neue Typographie‹ war der Titel

eines programmatischen Aufsatzes von Laszlo Moholy-Nagy im ›Bauhausbuch‹ 1923, das im Zusammenhang mit der ›Bauhaus-Ausstellung‹ in Weimar erschienen ist, die auch Jan Tschichold umgekehrt hat. Moholy-Nagy fordert darin »zuallererst: eindeutige Klarheit in allen typographischen Werken. Die Lesbarkeit – die Mitteilung darf nie unter einer a priori angenommenen Aesthetik leiden.

Die Buchstabentypen dürfen nie in eine vorbestimmte Form, z.B. ein Quadrat gezwängt werden.« Ein Jahr später, 1924, schreibt Moholy-Nagy seinen Aufsatz ›Zeitgemäße Typographie. Ziele, Praxis, Kritik und 1926 neben Aufsätzen zur Schriftform von Josef Albers und Herbert Bayer im Bauhaus-Sonderheft der Zeitschrift ›Offset‹. Schlagworte und Forderungen sind »Ausnutzung maschineller Möglichkeiten«, »Klarheit, Knappheit, Präzision«, »Einheitschrift, ohne Minuskeln und Majuskeln; nur Einheitsbuchstaben – nicht der Größe, sondern der Form nach.« Herbert Bayer läßt später auf die

Briefblätter des ›bauhaus dessau‹ in der Impressumszeile drucken: »wir schreiben alles klein, denn wir sparen damit zeite. Drei Monate nach der ›Offset‹-Nummer erscheint das Sonderheft

›elementare typographie‹ der ›Typo-

graphischen Mitteilungen‹, der Zeitschrift der Setzer und Drucker, herausge-

geben von Iwan Tschichold, »Typographie des Heftes: Ivan Tschichold, Leipzige. Sein einleitender Aufsatz ›Die Neue Gestaltung‹ nimmt die Methode des Buches ›Die Neue Typographie‹ vorweg. Tschichold referiert die Entwicklung der Avantgarde, insbesondere der Malerei der letzten Jahrzehnte und versucht, die neue Typographie als Ergebnis der »konsequenten Arbeit des russischen Suprematismus, des holländischen Neoplastizismus (De Stijl, G.F.) und insbesondere des Konstruktivismus darzustellen. »Neue Typographie« als Schlagwort und als Titel hatte zur Zeit des Erscheinens von

Tschicholds Buch schon Geschichte. ›Die Neue Typographie‹ war der Titel eines programmatischen Aufsatzes von Laszlo Moholy-Nagy im ›Bauhausbuch‹ 1923, das im Zusammenhang mit der ›Bauhaus-Ausstellung‹ in Weimar erschienen ist, die auch Jan Tschichold umgekehrt hat. Moholy-Nagy fordert darin »zuallererst: eindeutige Klarheit in allen typographischen Werken. Die Lesbarkeit – die Mitteilung darf nie unter einer a priori angenommenen Aesthetik leiden. Die Buchstabentypen dürfen nie in eine vorbestimmte

1 2 1 2

Editors, printers, designers, ophthalmologists, and

educators have been concerned with the legibility of print for more than a century. In the earlier years, there were many opinions and recommendati-

ons expressed on this subject; however, these were based on casual observation rather than upon research

findings. Prior to 1900, there were very few experimental studies reported, but since 1925, research in the field has expanded markedly. Before the nineteenth century, the main concern

was with esthetic appearance of print. With improved technology of printing, two additional factors entered the picture: Economy of printing and traditional practices. For many years, these three factors dominated the arrangement of the printed page. These emphases are still operating, although to a somewhat lesser degree. Because of these practices and views, a truly scientific typography

has been slow in developing. This discussion of legibility of print is concerned primarily with printed material to be read by adults. At what level do children read enough like adults so that it is not necessary to differentiate between the two in a discussion of the legibility of print? The results of two investigations provide an answer to this question. In a study of eye movements of children during reading, Buswell found a definite stabilization of the oculomotor patterns by the end of the 4th grade. In the second investigation, Ballantine discovered rapid gains in eye-movement efficiency

from the 2nd to the 4th grade and slower progress from the 4th to the 8th grade. Since oculomotor behavior represents efficiency in the mechanics of reading, one may conclude from these studies that the mechanics of

reading becomes well stabilized, or like that of adults, somewhere between the 4th and the 8th grades, i.e., between the ages of 10 and 13 years. This suggests that children read enough like adults so that typographical arrangements having optimal legibility for adults should also be optimal for children who are about 10 years of age or older. This is supported by some unpublished data of the writer. Editors, printers, designers, ophthalmologists, and educators have been concerned with the legibility of print for more than a century. In the earlier years, there were many opinions and recommendations expressed on this subject; however, these were based on

casual observation rather than upon research findings. Prior to 1900, there were very few experimental studies reported, but since 1925, research in the field has expanded markedly. Before the nineteenth century, the main concern was with esthetic appearance of print. With improved technology of printing, two additional factors entered the picture: Economy of printing and traditional practices. For many years, these three factors dominated the arrangement of the printed page. These emphases are still operating, although to a somewhat lesser degree. Because of these practices and views, a truly scientific typography has been slow in developing. This discussion of legibility of print is concerned primarily with printed material to be read by adults.

1 2 3

»Neue Typographie als Schlagwort und als Titel hatte

zur Zeit des Erscheinens von Tschicholds Buch schon Geschichte. ›Die Neue Typographie‹ war der Titel eines programmatischen Aufsatzes von Laszlo Moholy-Nagy im ›Bauhausbuch‹ 1923, das im Zusammenhang mit der ›Bauhaus-Ausstellung‹ in Weimar erschienen ist, die auch Jan Tschichold umgekehrt hat. Moholy-Nagy fordert darin »zuallererst: eindeutige Klarheit in allen typographischen Werken. Die Lesbarkeit – die Mitteilung darf nie unter einer a priori angenommenen Aesthetik leiden. Die Buchstabentypen dürfen nie in

eine vorbestimmte Form, z.B. ein Quadrat gezwängt werden.« Ein Jahr später, 1924, schreibt Moholy-Nagy seinen Aufsatz ›Zeitgemäße Typographie. Ziele,

Editors, printers, designers, ophthal mologists, and educa

tors have been concerned with the legibility of print for more than a century. In the earlier years, there were many opinions and recommendations expressed on this subject; however, these were based on casual observation rather than upon research findings. Prior to 1900, there were very few experimental studies reported, but since 1925, research in the field has expanded markedly. Before the nineteenth century, the main concern was with esthetic appearance of print.

With improved technology of printing, two additional factors entered the picture: Economy of printing and traditional practices. For many years, these three factors dominated the arrangement of the printed page. These emphases are still operating, although to a somewhat lesser degree. Because of these practices and views, a truly scientific typography has been slow

1 5 3 1 5 3

TYPOGRAPHY

358358

Variationen   **Variations**

Typografische Variationen sind Abwandlungen eines Themas, das heisst verschiedene Darstellungen desselben Inhalts. Der Kombination und Komposition sind je nach Inhalt kaum Grenzen gesetzt. Variieren heisst auch spielerisches Gestalten, heisst auch, die Möglichkeiten und Grenzen der Gestaltung mit Schrift zu erforschen. Voraussetzung ist, dass wir die typografischen Elemente kennen.

Typographical variations are modifications on a theme, i.e. different representations of the same content. Depending on the content, there are hardly any limits to the possibilities of combination and composition. Variation also means playful design and discovering the possibilities and boundaries of typography. Knowledge of the typographical elements is a necessary prerequisite for such experiments.

8 verschiedene Anordnungen desselben Textes in derselben Schrift auf gleichbleibender Fläche

8 different arrangements of the same text in the same type on a constant surface

Affiches anglaises
Musée des Beaux-Arts.
Jusqu'au 31 janvier 1972
107, rue de Rivoli, Paris

Affiches anglaises
Musée des Beaux-Arts. 107, rue de Rivoli
Paris , Jusqu'au 31 janvier 1972

Affiches anglaises	Musée des Beaux- Arts.	107, rue de Rivoli, Paris	Jusqu'au 31 janvier 1972

Affiches anglaises
Musée
des Beaux-Arts.
Jusqu'au 31 janvier 1972
107, rue de Rivoli,
Paris

Affiches	anglaises	Musée
des	Beaux-	Arts.
Jusqu'au	31	janvier
1972	107,	rue
de	Rivoli,	Paris

Affiches anglaises

Musée des Beaux-Arts.
107, rue de Rivoli, Paris

Jusqu'au 31 janvier 1972

Affiches
anglaises
Musée
des
Beaux-
Arts.
Jusqu'au
31
janvier
1972
107,
rue
de
Rivoli,
Paris

Affiches anglaises
Musée des Beaux-Arts.
Jusqu'au 31 janvier 1972
107, rue de Rivoli, Paris

Die Farbe der Typografie ist in der Regel Schwarz. Schwarz ist die dunkelste Farbe, hart, eher kalt, neutral. Schwarz ist einfach zu verarbeiten, zu ergänzen (Eindrucke, Nachdrucke).

Nur grosse Einzeltypen wirken wirklich schwarz. Bei einem Wort, einer Zeile und vor allem bei den Spalten mischt sich das Weiss der Zwischenräume mit den schwarzen Buchstabenformen zu Grau (optische Täuschung).

Die typografischen Grauwerte (heller oder dunkler) variieren nach Schriftform, Schriftgrösse, Schriftstärke, Schriftbreite, Buchstaben-, Wort- und Zeilenabständen.

Der Gestalter bestimmt den Grauwert einer typografischen Arbeit mit der Wahl und der Behandlung der Schrift. Eine fette Schrift wirkt dunkel, kann aber beispielsweise mit mehr Zeilenabstand in der Spalte aufgehellt werden.

Innerhalb einer gleichen Textgruppe ist nur ein ausgeglichener, ruhiger Grauton gut genug. Verschiedene Grautöne müssen sich deutlich voneinander unterscheiden.

The colour generally used for typographical work is black. Black is the darkest colour, hard, neutral and rather cold. Black is easy to handle and to use for additions such as imprinting and overprinting.

A truly black effect is obtained only with large single types. In a word, in a line and above all in columns, the white space intervening between the black characters produces the optical illusion of a grey effect.

Typographical grey effects, also known as ''colour'' (lighter or darker) vary with the form of the typeface, its size, weight and width and the amounts of letter spacing, word spacing and leading used.

The designer determines the grey value of the product through choice and treatment of type. For example, a bold type with dark appearance may be lightened by the use of more leading.

Within one block of text, a single, balanced and tranquil grey tone must be maintained. Different tones of grey must be clearly separated from one another.

Grauwerte der Univers:
mager, normal, halbfett, fett

Grey values of Univers:
light, regular, medium, bold

Editors, printers, designers, ophthalmologists, and educators have been concerned with the legibility of print for more than a century. In the earlier years, there were many opinions and recommendations expressed on this subject; however, these were based on casual observation rather than upon research findings. Prior to 1900, there were very few experimental studies reported, but since 1925, research in the field has expanded markedly. Before the nineteenth century, the main concern was with esthetic appearance of print. With improved technology of printing, two additional factors entered the picture: Economy of printing and traditional practices. For many years, these three factors dominated the arrangement of the printed page. These emphases are still operating,

»Neue Typographie« als Schlagwort und als Titel hatte zur Zeit des Erscheinens von Tschicholds Buch schon Geschichte. ›Die Neue Typographie‹ war der Titel eines programmatischen Aufsatzes von Laszlo Moholy-Nagy im ›Bauhausbuch‹ 1923, das im Zusammenhang mit der ›Bauhaus-Ausstellung‹ in Weimar erschienen ist, die auch Jan Tschichold umgekehrt hat. Moholy-Nagy fordert darin »zuallererst: eindeutige Klarheit in allen typographischen Werken. Die Lesbarkeit – die Mitteilung darf nie unter einer a priori angenommenen Ästhetik leiden. Die Buchstabentypen dürfen nie in eine vorbestimmte Form, z. B. ein Quadrat gezwängt werden.« Ein Jahr später, 1924, Schreibt Moholy-Nagy seinen Aufsatz ›Zeitgemäße Typographie. Ziele, Praxis, Kritik‹

Editors, printers, designers, ophthalmologists, and educators have been concerned with the legibility of print for more than a century. In the earlier years, there were many opinions and recommendations expressed on this subject; however, these were based on casual observation rather than upon research findings. Prior to 1900, there were very few experimental studies reported, but since 1925, research in the field has expanded markedly. Before the nineteenth century, the main concern was with esthetic appearance of print. With improved technology of printing, two additional factors entered the picture: Economy of printing and traditional practices. For many years,

»Neue Typographie« als Schlagwort und als Titel hatte zur Zeit des Erscheinens von Tschicholds Buch schon Geschichte. ›Die Neue Typographie‹ war der Titel eines programmatischen Aufsatzes von Laszlo Moholy-Nagy im ›Bauhausbuch‹ 1923, das im Zusammenhang mit der ›Bauhaus-Ausstellung‹ in Weimar erschienen ist, die auch Jan Tschichold umgekehrt hat. Moholy-Nagy fordert darin »zuallererst: eindeutige Klarheit in allen typographischen Werken. Die Lesbarkeit – die Mitteilung darf nie unter einer a priori angenommenen Ästhetik leiden. Die Buchstabentypen dürfen nie in eine vorbestimmte Form, z. B. ein Quadrat gezwängt werden.«

Farben

Jeder Farbton ist für typografische Arbeiten verwendbar, die sogenannt reinen Farben wie auch alle Mischtöne. Es gibt keine farbigen Texte, die in der richtigen Farbkombination und auf dem richtig ausgewählten Farbton der Grundfläche nicht lesbar sind.

Das Phänomen Farbe kann an dieser Stelle nicht behandelt werden. Damit haben sich Wissenschaftler und Künstler seit dem Altertum eingehend beschäftigt und ihre Erkenntnisse publiziert. Es können lediglich einige Stichworte gegeben werden, die auf die Anwendungsmöglichkeiten der Farbe in der Typografie hinweisen.

Farben als Ergänzung zur Form (und zu Schwarz, Weiss und Grau) bedeuten eine Erweiterung der visuellen Anziehungskraft.

Die Bestimmung der einzelnen Farben (Charakter) lässt sich bis heute nicht verbindlich festlegen. Doch gilt allgemein, dass die warmen Farben (Gelb, Orange, Rot) dynamisch, anregend, aggressiv; die kalten (Blau, Grün) ruhig, beruhigend und zurückhaltend wirken. Die warmen Farben kommen dem Betrachter entgegen, die kalten treten zurück.

Kontraste, Proportionen und Rhythmen spielen auch im Bereich der Farben eine primäre Rolle. Besondere Gegensätze der Farben sind warm und kalt, leuchtend und trüb, bunt und unbunt, Komplementär- und Simultankontraste.

Jeder Mensch empfindet Farbe individuell. Die Ausstrahlung einer Farbe oder einer Farbkombination wirkt deshalb immer verschieden.

Farbe kann rein funktionell eingesetzt werden, als Organisationshilfe zur Gliederung eines Textes (Titel oder Zahlen, die sich zum Beispiel in einer Farbe wiederholen; ganze Textgruppen, die sich durch ihre Farben unterscheiden), als Auszeichnung innerhalb eines Textes (einzelne Wörter oder Sätze),

Any colour may be used in typographical work, including all mixed hues as well as the so-called "pure" colours. If the right colour combinations are chosen and the colour of the paper is duly taken into account, text can be legible in any colour.

This is not the right place to go into the theory of colour, which has exercised scientists and artists since ancient times and on which a great deal has been published. We can only give a few maxims concerning the possibilities of using colour in typography.

Colours, as supplements to forms and to black, white and grey, provide an extension to the powers of visual attraction.

There has not yet been any final definition of the "character" of each colour, but it is generally true to say that warm colours (yellow, orange, red) have a dynamic, exciting, aggressive effect, while the cold colours (blue, green) have a tranquil, reassuring and restraining effect. Warm colours come forward to meet the viewer; cold colours hold back.

Contrasts, proportions and rhythms also play a leading part in the field of colours. Particular sets of opposites here are warm and cold, bright and dim, gaudy and restrained, complementary and simultaneous contrasts.

Each person has an individual colour sense, with the consequence that the radiance of a colour or combination of colours is seen differently by different people.

Colour can be used in a purely functional way, as an aid to the organization of a text: for example headings or figures may be repeatedly printed in a certain colour, or whole blocks of text may be differentiated by means of their colours. Colour may also be used for emphasizing single words or sentences within a text or as the mark of identification of the sponsor, where a certain colour

als Erkennungszeichen des Senders (eine bestimmte, sich wiederholende Farbe für eine bestimmte Institution).

Aufgrund der allgemeinen Bestimmung der Farben und der Farbtraditionen (die aber von Land zu Land verschieden sind) wissen wir, dass der Einsatz einer Farbe bestimmte Emotionen auslösen kann. Schwarz steht vielerorts für Trauer, wirkt vornehm, sachlich. Rot bedeutet Kraft, ist aggressiv, Symbol für Revolution.

Eine dritte Art der Farbanwendung ist jene, die die Farbe in erster Linie als ästhetisches Mittel einsetzt. Farbkombinationen, die als solche wirken, Farbordnungen nach logischen oder gefühlsmässigen Gesichtspunkten.

is repeatedly used for the name of a certain organization.

On the basis of generally accepted specifications and traditions in colour (which may vary from one country to another), we know that the use of a given hue can arouse certain emotions. Black is a sign of mourning in many parts of the world and has a distinguished and functional appearance. Red stands for power and is aggressive, a symbol of revolution.

A third way of using colour is to treat it primarily as an aesthetic medium, producing colour combinations which exist for their own sake, and colour arrangements from a standpoint of logic or feeling.

Typografische Masssysteme

Systems of Typographical Measurement

In der internationalen Praxis gibt es heute noch kein einheitliches Masssystem. Wir messen im Bereich der Typografie mit dem Didot-Punktsystem (in Europa), mit dem englisch-amerikanischen Pointsystem (in England, in den englischen Einflussgebieten und in Amerika), mit Millimetern (Metersystem) und mit Inches (Zollsystem). Die Vereinheitlichung ist aber nur noch eine Frage der Zeit.

Es sieht ganz so aus, als ob diese Vereinheitlichung im metrischen System realisiert werde. Es gilt zum Beispiel in allen Ländern der Europäischen Gemeinschaft seit 1978 (laut Gesetz über Einheiten und Messwesen) als typografisches Masssystem nur noch das metrische Masssystem.

In der Übergangszeit jedoch, in einer Zeit, wo je nach Ort und Satzproduzent alte (zum Beispiel Bleisatz) oder neue Satztechniken (zum Beispiel Fotosatz) angewendet werden, muss ein typografischer Gestalter die verschiedenen Masssysteme in den Grundzügen kennen.

Internationally, there is as yet no unified system of typographical measurement. Measurements are made in continental Europe with the Didot point system, in the English-speaking world with the British-American point system, and also in millimeters (metric system) and inches.

Unification is, however, only a matter of time, and it would appear that the metric system will be adopted. In all the countries of the European community, for example, the metric system has been the only official system of typographical measurement since the passing of the law on units and methods of measurement in 1978.

In the meantime, while both old typesetting methods (e.g. hot metal) and new ones (e.g. phototype) are being used by different suppliers in different places, a typographical designer must have a basic knowledge of the various systems of measurement.

Didot-Punktsystem

Kleinste ganze Einheit = 1 Punkt (0,376 mm)
12 Punkt (4,51 mm)   = 1 Cicero
                          in Deutschland,
                          Österreich und der
                          Schweiz
                          1 Douze
                          in Frankreich
                          1 Riga Tipografica
                          in Italien
                          1 Augustijn
                          in Holland

Didot Point System

Smallest whole unit = 1 point (0.376 mm)
12 points (4.51 mm) = 1 Cicero
                       in Germany, Austria
                       and Switzerland
                       1 Douze
                       in France
                       1 Riga Tipografica
                       in Italy
                       1 Augustijn
                       in the Netherlands

Englisch-amerikanisches Punktsystem

Kleinste ganze Einheit = 1 Point (0,351 mm)
12 Points (4,217 mm)   = 1 Pica
                         (oder Pica em)

British-American Point System

Smallest whole unit = 1 point (0.351 mm)
12 points (4.217 mm) = 1 Pica (or Pica em)

Metrisches System

Kleinste ganze Einheit	= 1 mm
10 mm	= 1 cm
100 mm	= 10 cm = 1 dm
1000 mm	= 100 cm = 10 dm
	= 1 m

Inch-System

Kleinste ganze Einheit	= 1 Inch (Zoll)
	= 25,4 mm
12 Inches	= 1 Foot
3 Feet	= 1 Yard

Vergleichszahlen (gerundete Werte)

1 mm	= 2,66 Didot-Punkt
	= 2,846 englisch-amerikanische Punkt
	= 0,0394 Inch
1 Didot-Punkt	= 0,376 mm
	= 1,07 englisch-amerikanische Punkt
	= 0,0148 Inch
1 englisch-amerikanischer Punkt	= 0,0138 Inch
	= 0,935 Didot-Punkt
	= 0,351 mm
1 Inch (Zoll)	= 72,291 englisch-amerikanische Punkt
	= 67,542 Didot-Punkt
	= 25,4 mm

Metric System

Smallest whole unit	= 1 mm
10 mm	= 1 cm
100 mm	= 10 cm = 1 dm
1000 mm	= 100 cm = 10 dm
	= 1 m

Inch System

Smallest whole unit	= 1 inch (25.4 mm)
12 inches	= 1 foot
3 feet	= 1 yard

Comparative Figures (rounded off)

1 mm	= 2.66 Didot points
	= 2.846 British-American points
	= 0.0394 inch
1 Didot point	= 0.376 mm
	= 1.07 British-American points
	= 0.0148 inch
1 British-American point	= 0.0138 inch
	= 0.935 Didot point
	= 0.351 mm
1 inch	= 72.291 British-American points
	= 67.542 Didot points
	= 25.4 mm

Didot-Punkt	mm	Brit.-Am. Points	Inches	Didot-Punkt	mm	Brit.-Am. Points	Inches
1	**0,376**	**1.070**	**0.0148**	**49**	18,419	52.425	0.7252
2	0,752	2.139	0.0296	50	18,785	53.495	0.7400
3	1,128	3.210	0.0444	51	19,171	54.565	0.7548
4	1,504	4.280	0.0592	52	19,547	55.635	0.7696
5	1,879	5.349	0.0740	53	19,923	56.705	0.7844
6	2,255	6.419	0.0888	54	20,299	57.775	0.7992
7	2,631	7.489	0.1036	55	20,675	58.845	0.8140
8	3,007	8.559	0.1184	56	21,050	59.915	0.8288
9	3,383	9.629	0.1332	57	21,426	60.984	0.8436
10	3,759	10.699	0.1480	58	21,802	62.054	0.8584
11	4,135	11.769	0.1628	59	22,178	63.124	0.8732
12	4,511	12.839	0.1776	60	22,554	64.194	0.8880
13	4,887	13.909	0.1924	61	22,929	65.264	0.9028
14	5,263	14.979	0.2072	62	23,306	66.334	0.9176
15	5,638	16.049	0.2220	63	23,682	67.404	0.9324
16	6,014	17.118	0.2368	64	24,058	68.473	0.9472
17	6,390	18.188	0.2516	65	24,434	69.544	0.9620
18	6,766	19.258	0.2664	66	24,809	70.613	0.9768
19	7,142	20.328	0.2812	67	25,185	71.683	0.9916
20	7,518	21.398	0.2960	68	25,561	72.753	1.0064
21	7,894	22.468	0.3108	69	25,937	73.823	1.0212
22	8,270	23.539	0.3256	70	26,313	74.893	1.0360
23	8,646	24.608	0.3404	71	26,689	75.962	1.0508
24	9,023	25.678	0.3552	72	27,065	77.032	1.0656
25	9,398	26.748	0.3700	73	27,441	78.103	1.0804
26	9,773	27.814	0.3848	74	27,817	79.173	1.0952
27	10,149	28.887	0.3996	75	28,193	80.243	1.1100
28	10,525	29.957	0.4144	76	28,568	81.312	1.1248
29	10,901	31.027	0.4292	77	28,944	82.382	1.1396
30	11,277	32.097	0.4440	78	29,320	83.452	1.1544
31	11,653	33.167	0.4588	79	29,696	84.522	1.1692
32	12,029	34.237	0.4736	80	30,072	85.592	1.1840
33	12,405	35.307	0.4884	81	30,448	86.661	1.1988
34	12,781	36.377	0.5032	82	30,824	87.732	1.2136
35	13,157	37.447	0.5180	83	31,199	88.801	1.2284
36	13,532	38.516	0.5328	84	31,577	89.871	1.2432
37	13,908	39.586	0.5476	96	36,088	102.710	1.4208
38	14,284	40.656	0.5624				
39	14,660	41.726	0.5772	108	40,599	115.548	1.5984
40	15,036	42.796	0.5920				
41	15,412	43.866	0.6068	120	45,110	128.387	1.7760
42	15,788	44.936	0.6216				
43	16,164	46.007	0.6364	132	49,621	141.226	1.9536
44	16,539	47.077	0.6512				
45	16,916	48.146	0.6660	144	54,132	154.065	2.1312
46	17,291	49.215	0.6808				
47	17,667	50.285	0.6956				
48	18,043	51.355	0.7104				

mm	Didot-Punkt	Inches	Brit.-Am. Points	mm	Didot-Punkt	Inches	Brit.-Am. Points
0,25	0,665	0.0099	0.712	**12,25**	32,573	0.4827	34.864
0,50	1,330	0.0197	1.423	**12,50**	33,238	0.4925	35.575
0,75	1,994	0.0296	2.135	**12,75**	33,902	0.5024	36.287
1,00	**2,659**	**0.0394**	**2.846**	**13,00**	34,567	0.5122	36.998
1,25	3,324	0.0493	3.558	**13,25**	35,232	0.5221	37.710
1,50	3,989	0.0591	4.269	**13,50**	35,897	0.5319	38.421
1,75	4,653	0.0690	4.981	**13,75**	36,561	0.5418	39.133
2,00	5,318	0.0788	5.692	**14,00**	37,226	0.5516	39.844
2,25	5,983	0.0887	6.404	**14,25**	37,891	0.5615	40.556
2,50	6,648	0.0985	7.115	**14,50**	38,556	0.5713	41.267
2,75	7,312	0.1084	7.827	**14,75**	39,220	0.5812	41.979
3,00	7,977	0.1182	8.538	**15,00**	39,885	0.5910	42.690
3,25	8,642	0.1281	9.250	**15,25**	40,550	0.6009	43.402
3,50	9,307	0.1379	9.961	**15,50**	41,215	0.6107	44.113
3,75	9,971	0.1478	10.673	**15,75**	41,879	0.6206	44.825
4,00	10,636	0.1576	11.384	**16,00**	42,544	0.6304	45.536
4,25	11,301	0.1675	12.096	**16,25**	43,209	0.6403	46.248
4,50	11,966	0.1773	12.807	**16,50**	43,874	0.6501	46.959
4,75	12,630	0.1872	13.519	**16,75**	44,538	0.6600	47.671
5,00	13,295	0.1970	14.230	**17,00**	45,203	0.6698	48.382
5,25	13,960	0.2069	14.942	**17,25**	45,868	0.6797	49.094
5,50	14,625	0.2167	15.653	**17,50**	46,533	0.6895	49.805
5,75	15,289	0.2266	16.365	**17,75**	47,197	0.6994	50.517
6,00	15,954	0.2364	17.076	**18,00**	47,862	0.7092	51.228
6,25	16,619	0.2463	17.788	**18,25**	48,527	0.7191	51.940
6,50	17,284	0.2561	18.499	**18,50**	49,192	0.7289	52.651
6,75	17,948	0.2660	19.211	**18,75**	49,856	0.7388	53.363
7,00	18,613	0.2758	19.922	**19,00**	50,521	0.7486	54.074
7,25	19,278	0.2857	20.634	**19,25**	51,186	0.7585	54.786
7,50	19,943	0.2955	21.345	**19,50**	51,851	0.7683	55.497
7,75	20,607	0.3054	22.057	**19,75**	52,515	0.7782	56.209
8,00	21,272	0.3152	22.768	**20,00**	53,180	0.7880	56.920
8,25	21,937	0.3251	23.480				
8,50	22,602	0.3349	24.191				
8,75	23,266	0.3448	24.903				
9,00	23,931	0.3546	25.614				
9,25	24,596	0.3645	26.326				
9,50	25,261	0.3743	27.037				
9,75	25,925	0.3842	27.749				
10,00	26,590	0.3940	28.460				
10,25	27,255	0.4039	29.172				
10,50	27,920	0.4137	29.883				
10,75	28,584	0.4236	30.595				
11,00	29,249	0.4334	31.306				
11,25	29,914	0.4433	32.018				
11,50	30,579	0.4531	32.729				
11,75	31,243	0.4630	33.441				
12,00	31,908	0.4728	34.152				

Brit.-Am. Points	Inches	Didot-Punkt	mm	Brit.-Am. Points	Inches	Didot-Punkt	mm
1	**0.0138**	**0,935**	**0,351**	49	0.6778	45,795	17,219
2	0.0276	1,869	0,703	50	0.6916	46,730	17,570
3	0.0415	2,804	1,054	51	0.7054	47,665	17,921
4	0.0553	3,738	1,406	52	0.7193	48,599	18,273
5	0.0690	4,673	1,757	53	0.7331	49,534	18,624
6	0.0830	5,608	2,108	54	0.7470	50,468	18,976
7	0.0968	6,542	2,460	55	0.7608	51,403	19,327
8	0.1107	7,477	2,811	56	0.7746	52,338	19,678
9	0.1245	8,411	3,163	57	0.7885	53,272	20,030
10	0.1383	9,346	3,514	58	0.8023	54,207	20,381
11	0.1521	10,281	3,865	59	0.8161	55,141	20,733
12	0.1660	11,215	4,217	60	0.8301	56,076	21,084
13	0.1798	12,150	4,568	61	0.8438	57,011	21,435
14	0.1936	13,084	4,920	62	0.8576	57,945	21,787
15	0.2074	14,019	5,271	63	0.8715	58,880	22,138
16	0.2213	14,954	5,622	64	0.8853	59,814	22,490
17	0.2351	15,888	5,974	65	0.8991	60,749	22,841
18	0.2490	16,823	6,325	66	0.9130	61,684	23,192
19	0.2628	17,757	6,677	67	0.9268	62,618	23,544
20	0.2766	18,692	7,028	68	0.9406	63,553	23,895
21	0.2904	19,627	7,379	69	0.9545	64,487	24,247
22	0.3043	20,561	7,731	70	0.9683	65,422	24,598
23	0.3181	21,496	8,082	71	0.9821	66,357	24,949
24	0.3320	22,430	8,434	72	0.9960	67,291	25,301
25	0.3458	23,365	8,785	73	1.0098	68,225	25,652
26	0.3596	24,230	9,136	74	1.0236	69,160	26,004
27	0.3734	25,234	9,488	75	1.0375	70,095	26,355
28	0.3873	26,169	9,839	76	1.0513	71,030	26,706
29	0.4011	27,103	10,191	77	1.0651	71,964	27,058
30	0.4150	28,038	10,542	78	1.0790	72,899	27,409
31	0.4288	28,973	10,893	79	1.0930	73,933	27,761
32	0.4426	29,907	11,245	80	1.1066	74,768	28,112
33	0.4564	30,842	11,596	81	1.1205	75,703	28,463
34	0.4703	31,776	11,948	82	1.1343	76,637	28,815
35	0.4841	32,711	12,299	83	1.1481	77,572	29,166
36	0.4980	33,646	12,650	84	1.1620	78,506	29,518
40	0.5533	37,384	14,056	96	1.3280	89,721	33,735
41	0.5671	38,319	14,407				
42	0.5810	39,253	14,759	108	1.4940	100,936	37,952
43	0.5948	40,188	15,110	120	1.6600	112,151	42,169
44	0.6086	41,122	15,462				
45	0.6224	42,057	15,813				
46	0.6363	42,992	16,164	132	1.8260	123,367	46,385
47	0.6501	43,926	16,516				
48	0.6640	44,861	16,867	144	1.9920	134,582	50,602

Inches	Brit.-Am. Points	mm	Didot-Punkt	Inches	Brit.-Am. Points	mm	Didot-Punkt
1/32	2.259	0,794	2,111	1 17/32	110.696	38,894	103,424
2/32	4.518	1,588	4,221	1 18/32	112.955	39,688	105,534
3/32	6.777	2,381	6,332	1 19/32	115.214	40,481	107,645
4/32	9.036	3,175	8,443	1 20/32	117.473	41,275	109,756
5/32	11.295	3,969	10,553	1 21/32	119.732	42,069	111,866
6/32	13.555	4,763	12,664	1 22/32	121.991	42,863	113,977
7/32	15.814	5,556	14,775	1 23/32	124.250	43,656	116,088
8/32	18.073	6,350	16,886	1 24/32	126.509	44,450	118,199
9/32	20.332	7,144	18,996	1 25/32	128.768	45,244	120,309
10/32	22.591	7,938	21,107	1 26/32	131.027	46,038	122,420
11/32	24.850	8,731	23,218	1 27/32	133.287	46,831	124,531
12/32	27.109	9,525	25,328	1 28/32	135.546	47,625	126,641
13/32	29.368	10,319	27,439	1 29/32	137.805	48,419	128,752
14/32	31.627	11,113	29,550	1 30/32	140.064	49,213	130,863
15/32	33.886	11,906	31,660	1 31/32	142.323	50,006	132,973
16/32	36.146	12,700	33,771	2	144.582	50,800	135,084
17/32	38.405	13,494	35,882				
18/32	40.664	14,288	37,992				
19/32	42.923	15,081	40,103				
20/32	45.182	15,875	42,214				
21/32	47.441	16,669	44,324				
22/32	49.700	17,463	46,435				
23/32	51.959	18,256	48,546				
24/32	54.218	19,050	50,657				
25/32	56.477	19,844	52,767				
26/32	58.736	20,638	54,878				
27/32	60.996	21,431	56,989				
28/32	63.255	22,225	59,099				
29/32	65.514	23,019	61,210				
30/32	67.773	23,813	63,321				
31/32	70.032	24,606	65,431				
1	**72.291**	**25,400**	**67,542**				
1 1/32	74.550	26,194	69,653				
1 2/32	76.809	26,988	71,763				
1 3/32	79.068	27,781	73,874				
1 4/32	81.327	28,575	75,985				
1 5/32	83.586	29,369	78,095				
1 6/32	85.846	30,163	80,206				
1 7/32	88.105	30,956	82,317				
1 8/32	90.364	31,750	84,428				
1 9/32	92.623	32,544	86,538				
1 10/32	94.882	33,338	88,649				
1 11/32	97.141	34,131	90,760				
1 12/32	99.400	34,925	92,870				
1 13/32	101.659	35,719	94,981				
1 14/32	103.918	36,513	97,092				
1 15/32	106.177	37,306	99,202				
1 16/32	108.437	38,100	101,313				

Messtechnik vertikal

Bleisatz

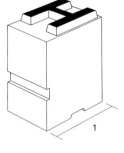

Im Bleisatz (gegossene Satzelemente) werden alle Dimensionen in Punkt (Didot- oder englisch-amerikanische Punkt) gemessen. Das Mass des Kegels (1) wird als Schriftgrad (Schriftgrösse) angegeben. Das sichtbare Schriftbild ist kleiner, die Versalhöhen variieren von Schrift zu Schrift (2). Der Zeilenabstand entspricht bei kompressem Satz dem Schriftkegel und wird von Fusslinie zu Fusslinie (4) oder von Kopflinie zu Kopflinie (3) gemessen.

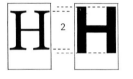

Zusätzliche Abstände zwischen den Zeilen nennen wir Durchschuss. Der Durchschuss im Bleisatz (Blindmaterial) misst 1 Punkt, 2 Punkt, 3 Punkt, 4 Punkt, 6 Punkt.

Fotosatz

Im Fotosatz werden je nach Hersteller und System die Masse in Punkt oder Millimetern angegeben. Das Messprinzip ist grundsätzlich dasselbe wie im Bleisatz. Die Schriftgrössen beziehen sich auf einen fiktiven Schriftkegel oder Mindestzeilenabstand. Auch hier ist das sichtbare Schriftbild kleiner als der Zeilenabstand, und die Versalhöhen variieren von Schrift zu Schrift.
Zusätzlicher Durchschuss zwischen den Zeilen ist im Fotosatz je nach Hersteller in Punkt oder Millimetern (zum Beispiel in 0,25-mm-Schritten) angegeben. Gemessen wird der Zeilenabstand wie im Bleisatz von Fusslinie zu Fusslinie (4) oder von Kopflinie zu Kopflinie (3).

Das vertikale Mass des Kegels im Bleisatz wie auch der Mindestzeilenabstand im Fotosatz umfassen die gesamte vertikale Höhe einer Zeile, einschliesslich eines kleinen Abstandes, damit Ober- und Unterlängen der Buchstaben nicht aneinanderstossen.

Vertical Measurements

Metal Setting

In metal setting with cast pieces, all dimensions are measured in points, whether Didot or British-American. The body size (1) is given as the type size, although the visible type image is smaller and the capital height often varies considerably from one typeface to another (2). In solid-set text, the distance between lines is equal to the body size and is measured from baseline to base-line (4) or from cap line to cap line (3).

Additional spacing between lines is known as "leading", from the lead spacing material used in metal setting, measured as 1 point, 2 points, 3 points, 4 points, 6 points.

Photosetting

In photosetting the measurements are given either in points or in millimeters, depending on the system and the manufacturer. The principle of measurement is basically the same as for metal types. The type sizes relate to a supposed type body, which includes the minimum space between lines. Here too, the visible type image is smaller than the body size and capital letter height varies from face to face.
Additional interlinear space in photosetting (leading), is specified in points or mm (e.g. steps of 0.25 mm), depending on the manufacturer. The distance between lines is measured, as in metal setting, from baseline to baseline (4) or cap line to cap line (3).

The vertical measurement of the type body in metal setting and the minimum space between the lines in photosetting incorporate the total depth of a line, including a small interval to prevent the descenders from touching the ascenders of the line below.

Messtechnik horizontal

Horizontal Measurements

Bleisatz

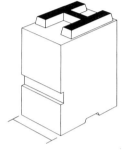

Im Bleisatz werden die gegossenen Buchstaben einzeln aneinandergereiht. Die Breite (Dickte) enthält den Raumbedarf des Buchstabens einschliesslich eines kleinen Abstandes, damit die einzelnen Buchstaben sich nicht berühren. Zusätzliche Abstände zwischen den einzelnen Buchstaben und die Abstände zwischen den Wörtern werden in Punkt und in Gevierten angegeben. Diese Zwischenräume nennt man Ausschluss. Das durch den Ausschluss bestimmte Wortbild bezeichnen wir mit normal (ohne Ausschluss), weit, sehr weit oder gesperrt. Enger als normal kann im Bleisatz nicht gesetzt werden.

Ausschlussstücke im Didot-Punktsystem:

¼ Punkt
½ Punkt
1 Punkt
1½ Punkt
2 Punkt
3 Punkt
4 Punkt

¼ Geviert
⅓ Geviert
½ Geviert
⅟₁ Geviert (Quadrat der Schriftgrösse, zum Beispiel 12×12 Punkt)

Metal Setting

In metal setting the cast characters are lined up individually. Their width (set) comprises the space required for the letter plus a small addition to prevent the letters from touching each other. Extra spacing between letters and the distances between words are denoted in points and em quads and are known as letter spacing and word spacing. The word image determined by the spacing may be normal (no extra spacing), loose or very loose. With metal types it is not possible to set the letters closer together than the normal distance.

Spacing material in American-British points:

¼ point (stainless steel)
½ point (copper)
1 point

⅙ em
⅕ em
¼ em
⅓ em
½ em
1 em (em quad of type size, e.g. 12×12 points)

Fotosatz

Im Fotosatz werden die Breiten der Buchstaben und die Wortabstände mit Einheiten gemessen. Diese Einheit ist im Gegensatz zum Punkt keine feste Grösse. Die Einheit ist Teil des Gevierts, das heisst des Quadrates mit dem Mindestzeilenabstand als Seitenmass. Das Geviert wird zum Beispiel in 18 gleich grosse Einheiten geteilt. Die Grösse der Einheiten variiert entsprechend der Grösse der Schrift. Diese Grundeinteilung des Gevierts kann je nach Fabrikat auch weiter (zum Beispiel mit 16 Einheiten) oder enger (zum Beispiel mit 48 Einheiten) sein.

Für jedes System und für jede Schrift sind eine Normalschriftweite (Buchstabenabstand) und entsprechende Normalwortabstände nach dem Prinzip der optimalen Lesbarkeit bestimmt. Von dieser «Norm» sollte der Gestalter nur in begründeten Fällen abweichen (sehr kurze Zeilen, Negativsatz, spezieller Titelsatz).

Für die Bestimmung der Schriftweiten stehen uns zum Beispiel folgende Masse und Begriffe zur Verfügung (Berthold):

+ 2 sehr weit
+ 1 weit
± 0 normal
− 1 eng
− 2 sehr eng

Zur Bestimmung der Spaltenbreiten verwenden wir Punkt und Cicero oder Millimeter.

Theoretische Kenntnisse im Bereich der typografischen Masse allein garantieren kaum erfolgreiche Resultate in der Praxis. Vor allem jungen Gestaltern mit noch wenig Erfahrung wird empfohlen, sich eine ausgewählte kleine Schriftmusterbibliothek anzuschaffen. Die Schriftmuster helfen entscheidend mit, die richtige Wahl zu treffen und in der Folge die Satzbestellungen eindeutig mit den richtigen Massen zu versehen.

Photosetting

In photosetting the character widths and word spacing are measured in units. Unlike the point, the unit has no fixed size, being a fraction of the em quad, that is of the square with a side equal to the minimum line depth. The em may be divided into 18 equal units, the size of which varies in accordance with the size of the typeface. Some manufacturers divide the em into larger units, totalling 16, and others work to smaller units, up to 48 per em.

For every system and every typeface, a normal character set-width and a correspondingly normal word spacing is determined by the principle of optimum legibility. The designer should not depart from this norm except in special instances, such as very short lines, reversed white on black setting or special kinds of display line.

The following measurements and terms are available for the determination of letter spacing (e.g. Berthold):

+ 2 very loose
+ 1 loose
± 0 normal
− 1 tight
− 2 very tight

We define column widths in points and picas, or inches or millimeters.

Theoretical knowledge alone can hardly guarantee successful practical results in the field of typographical measurements. Young designers with little experience are recommended to collect a small selection of type-specimen sheets and books. These will be of decisive aid in making the right choice and clearly marking up typesetting orders with the correct measurements.

Je besser das Manuskript für den Setzer vor-
bereitet ist, um so eher ist die Garantie einer
reibungslosen und kostensparenden Produktion gegeben. Nicht zu verwechseln ist
die Manuskriptbearbeitung mit der technischen Arbeitsvorbereitung. (Die technische
Arbeitsvorbereitung wird vom Produktions-
betrieb besorgt.)

Die Entwicklung in der Satzherstellung ver-
langt heute einen rationellen Arbeitsablauf.
Voraussetzung dafür sind die einwandfreie
Textkorrektur und genaue Satzanweisungen.

Das Manuskript

Ein Manuskript wird vom Autor mit der
Schreibmaschine getippt oder mit einem
Texterfassungssystem über den Bildschirm
auf einer Diskette erfasst. Handschriftliche
Manuskripte sind zu vermeiden.

Ein Schreibmaschinenmanuskript soll immer
mit doppelter Zeilenschaltung geschrieben
werden. Damit ist das Manuskript leicht
lesbar. Allfällige Handkorrekturen sind pro-
blemlos einzufügen.

Ist die typografische Gestaltung schon bei
der Herstellung des Manuskriptes bekannt,
so soll die Anzahl der Buchstaben pro Manu-
skriptzeile der Anzahl der Buchstaben einer
gesetzten Zeile entsprechen. Damit kann der
Umfang des gesetzten Textes schon vor der
Satzherstellung bemessen werden (wichtig
für genaue Umbruchentwürfe).

Im Moment der Übergabe eines Manuskriptes bzw. einer Diskette an den Setzer
müssen diese so verbindlich wie nur irgend
möglich sein. Satzkorrekturen werden je
nach Umfang sehr kostspielig und zeitrau-
bend.

The more carefully the manuscript is prepared for the typesetter, the better is the
guarantee of trouble-free and economical
production. Copy preparation is not to be
confused with the technical preparations
for production which are undertaken by the
typesetting service or department.

A rational sequence of operations is required
for typesetting by modern methods, for
which two of the essential conditions are
careful checking of the text and precise instructions for the typesetter.

The Manuscript

A manuscript for typesetting is usually either
typewritten by the author or written on to a
floppy disc by means of a word-processing
system with display screen. Handwritten
manuscripts should be avoided.

A typescript should always be typed with
double line spacing. This makes it easy to
read and leaves room for the insertion of any
required corrections.

If the typographical design of the work has
already been established at the time when
the manuscript is produced, it should be
typed with the same number of characters
per line as will appear in the typeset line.
This enables the extent of the typeset text to
be measured before typesetting begins and
is an important aid to precise layout and
pagination.

When a typed manuscript or floppy disc is
delivered to the typesetter, it must as far as
possible be regarded as final and binding.
Depending on their extent, author's corrections to typesetting can be very expensive
and time-consuming.

Manuskriptkorrektur

Die Manuskriptkorrektur umfasst die klare Bezeichnung aller gewünschten Zusätze, sprachlichen Änderungen und orthographischen Korrekturen mit den landesüblichen Korrekturzeichen (fremdsprachige Texte sind speziell sorgfältig durchzusehen).

Einfügungen und Änderungen in Ergänzung zu den Korrekturzeichen sind nicht zwischen die Zeilen zu schreiben, sondern immer links vom Manuskripttext anzubringen.

Eine Korrektur klärt alle Fragen der einheitlichen Schreibweise und andere sprachliche Probleme.

Satzanweisungen

Für die Satzherstellung sind folgende Satzanweisungen deutlich und lückenlos anzugeben:

- Satztechnik (zum Beispiel Bleisatz oder Fotosatz)

- Satzprodukt
  Bleisatz:
  Korrekturabzug oder reprofähiger Abzug auf Kunstdruckpapier
  Fotosatz:
  Papierkopie positiv oder negativ
  Siebdruckfilm positiv oder negativ
  Offsetfilm positiv oder negativ
  Dünnfilm seitenrichtig oder seitenverkehrt
  Stripfilm selbstklebend
  Color-Key

- Schrifttyp/en (Schriftname, zum Beispiel Univers)
- Schriftgrössen (zum Beispiel 12 Punkt)
- Schriftstärken (zum Beispiel mager)
- Schriftbreiten (zum Beispiel schmal)
- Schriftlagen (normal oder kursiv)

Manuscript Correction

Manuscript correction includes clear indication of all required additions, changes to words and punctuation and spelling corrections, using the correction signs accepted in the country of production. Special care is required for checking foreign-language texts.

Insertions and alterations supplementary to the correction marks must not be written between the lines of the manuscript but in its left-hand margin.

A correction of the manuscript should clear up all questions of consistent spelling and other linguistic problems.

Typesetting Instructions (Mark-up)

The manuscript must be clearly and fully marked up for typesetting with the following instructions:

- Typesetting technique (e.g. metal or photosetting)

- Typesetting product
  Metalsetting:
  Proof for correction or reproduction proof on paper of good quality
  Photosetting:
  Positive or negative paper copy
  Positive or negative film for screen process printing
  Positive or negative film for offset-litho printing
  Right-reading or reverse-reading thin film
  Self-adhesive stripping film
  Color-Key

- Typeface/s (name of typeface, e.g. Univers)
- Type sizes (e.g. 12 points)
- Type weights (e.g. light)
- Type widths (e.g. condensed)
- Type angles (roman or italic)

- Buchstabenabstand (Schriftweite)
  Bleisatz:
  normal oder gesperrt
  Fotosatz:
  zum Beispiel ± 0 oder −1 oder +1

- Spaltenbreiten (zum Beispiel 60 mm oder 12 Cicero)
- Spaltenarten (Flatter-, Blocksatz oder Mittelachse)
- Zeilenfall (gemäss Spaltenbreite oder wie Manuskript)
- Zeilenabstand
  Bleisatz:
  kompress oder zusätzlicher Abstand in Punkt (zum Beispiel 12/14 Punkt)
  Fotosatz:
  Mindestzeilenabstand oder grösserer Zeilenabstand in mm (zum Beispiel 12 Punkt / 5 mm)

- Trennart (mit oder ohne Silbentrennung)

Satzanweisungen im Manuskript haben sich eindeutig von diesem zu unterscheiden, in der Schreibweise wie in der Farbe (rot). Satzanweisungen, welche sich oft wiederholen, sind mit Nummern oder Farben zu codieren und auf einem separaten Blatt zu erklären.

Satzanweisungen für die elektronische Textverarbeitung sind über das entsprechende System einzugeben. Die Anweisungen bleiben grundsätzlich dieselben, nur die Technik ist anders.

Satzanweisungs- und Korrekturzeichen

Diese Zeichen unterscheiden sich von Land zu Land. Die gebräuchlichen Zeichen sind in der Regel in allen Satzmusterbüchern enthalten und sind bei den Herstellern erhältlich.

- Set-width of letters
  Metalsetting:
  Normal or spaced out
  Photosetting:
  E.g. ±0 or −1 or +1

- Column width (e.g. 60 mm or 12 pica ems or Cicero)
- Style of column (unjustified, justified or centered)
- Line length (as column width or as typed)
- Leading (interlinear spacing)
  Metalsetting:
  Set solid or with additional leading in points (e.g. 12/14 points)
  Photosetting:
  Minimum line depth or extra spacing in mm (e.g. 12 points / 5 mm)

- Hyphenation style (with or without word breaks)

The manuscript mark-up must be clearly distinguished from the text by its manner of writing and colour (red). Any instructions which recur frequently may be coded as numbers or colours and explained on a separate sheet.

Typesetting instructions for electronic text processing must be input through the system concerned. The mark-up is basically the same, only the technique is different.

Mark-up and Correction Signs

These signs vary from one country to another. The accepted signs are usually included in all type specimen books and are available from the suppliers.

**Inventory of
Typesetting Technics**
by Jürg Fritzsche

Die Kunst des Druckens – die Schwarze Kunst – ist in Europa seit etwa 1400 bekannt. Damals wurden sogenannte Einblattdrucke hergestellt. Das sind religiöse Bilder, in Holzplatten geschnitten, mit schwarzer Farbe eingefärbt und auf Papier abgerieben. Die Druckerpresse war noch nicht erfunden, ebenso waren Buchstaben, mit denen man Wörter zusammensetzen kann, noch unbekannt. Bücher, bei denen Bild und Schrift in Holztafeln geschnitten und deren Blätter nur einseitig bedruckt wurden, nennt man Blockbücher.

The art of printing—the "Black Art"—has been known in Europe since about 1400 AD. At that time, single-sheet prints of religious pictures were produced from woodcuts, which were given a coating of black ink that was transferred to paper. The printing press had not yet been invented and there was still no knowledge of printing types with which words could be assembled. Books of the period, consisting of pages printed on one side only from woodcuts combining lettering with illustration, are known as "block books".

Die Vorläufer der Druckkunst

Die alten Kulturvölker des Vorderen Orients, die Babylonier und Assyrer, drückten mit Griffeln Schriftzeichen in Ton ein, den sie nachher brannten. Die Ägypter meisselten ihre Schriftzeichen (Hieroglyphen) in Stein; etwa vom 3. vorchristlichen Jahrtausend an schrieben sie auf Papyrus, das in Europa noch bis ins Jahr 1000 n.Chr. verwendet wurde. Die Griechen und Römer meisselten ebenfalls in Stein; später verwendeten sie Papyrus, und etwa im 2. vorchristlichen Jahrhundert wurde das Pergament erfunden. Das Papier wurde in Europa erst im 12. Jahrhundert bekannt. Sein Ursprungsland ist China, wo die Anfänge der Papierherstellung etwa ins 2. oder 3. vorchristliche Jahrhundert zurückgehen. Sichere Kunde hat man aber erst aus dem Jahre 105 n.Chr. von einem Papierschöpfer mit Namen Tsai Lun. Die erste Papiermühle in Europa wurde im 12. Jahrhundert bei Valencia in Spanien gegründet.

Forerunners of Printing

The ancient civilizations of the Middle East, in Babylon and Assyria, used a stylus to impress characters into clay, which was subsequently baked. The Egyptians chiselled their characters (hieroglyphs) in stone and, from about the 3rd millenium BC, wrote them on papyrus, a material that continued to be used in Europe up to the beginning of the 2nd millenium AD. The Greeks and Romans also engraved their lettering in stone, later using papyrus, and parchment was invented probably in the 2nd century BC. Paper was unknown in Europe until the 12th century. Its land of origin is China, where the beginnings of papermaking probably date back to the 2nd or 3rd century BC, although the first certain evidence dates from 105 AD and relates to a papermaker named Tsai Lun. The first papermill in Europe was established in the 12th century near Valencia in Spain.

Gutenberg

Während Jahrhunderten schufen Mönche in den Klöstern und später auch weltliche Schreiber handgeschriebene Bücher auf Pergament, die mit Initialen, Miniaturen und Randverzierungen ausgeschmückt wurden.

Gutenberg

For centuries, cloistered monks and later on lay scribes penned handwritten books on parchment, embellishing them with decorative initials, miniature paintings and marginal ornaments. For the young nobleman of

Diese Bücher waren für den Junker Johann Gensfleisch zum Gutenberg aus Mainz die Vorbilder für seine gedruckten Bücher.

Die Bücher des Mittelalters waren den Gelehrten vorbehalten. Das Analphabetentum überwog bis ins 17. Jahrhundert. Ausserdem waren die handgeschriebenen Bücher auf Pergament für die weite Verbreitung zu teuer. Daran änderte sich auch nichts, als sich die Papiermacherkunst in Europa ausdehnte.

Papier war aber die notwendige Voraussetzung für eine Erfindung, die als eine der wesentlichsten der Weltgeschichte anzusehen ist: die Erfindung des Buchdrucks. Die Erfindung Gutenbergs (1440) war eine Revolution – und doch bestand sie «nur» in technischen Neuerungen: Er liess sich von Konrad Saspach eine Druckerpresse bauen, erdachte das System des Setzens mit Einzelbuchstaben und erfand ein Instrument zum Giessen von Bleilettern. Gutenberg war also zugleich Schriftgiesser, Schriftsetzer und Buchdrucker. Damit war der Grundstein zur industriellen Fertigung von Druckerzeugnissen gelegt.

Es ist bemerkenswert, dass nicht nur die Papierherstellung, sondern auch der Holztafeldruck und das Einzelbuchstabensystem in China viel früher bekannt waren. Das älteste gedruckte Buch, die Diamond Sutra, wurde im Jahre 868 n.Chr. gedruckt. Um etwa 1050 wurden aus gebranntem Ton zusammensetzbare Schriftzeichen hergestellt. In Korea waren Typen aus Metall nachweisbar bereits im Jahre 1392 bekannt.

Handsatz

Jahrhundertelang war der Handsatz das einzige Verfahren zur Satzherstellung. Sein Prinzip: Einzelne Lettern aus Blei werden zu einer Zeile zusammengefügt. Die Zeilen aneinandergereiht, ergänzt durch Blindmate-

Mainz, Johann Gensfleisch zum Gutenberg, such books were models for his printed products.

The books of the Middle Ages were reserved for the learned. General illiteracy prevailed until the 17th century, and in any case handwritten books on parchment were too expensive for wide distribution. This situation did not change even when papermaking spread through Europe.

Paper was, however, the necessary condition for an invention which may be regarded as one of the most important in world history: letterpress printing. Gutenberg's invention (1440) was revolutionary, and yet it consisted "only" of technical innovations. Gutenberg had his printing press built by Konrad Saspach. He worked out the system of setting with single types and invented equipment for the casting of letters in lead. Thus he was at the same time a typefounder, a typesetter and a printer, laying the foundation stone for the industrial production of printed matter.

It is a remarkable fact that not only papermaking but also wood-block engraving and movable types were known much earlier in China. The oldest printed book, the Diamond Sutra, dates from 868 AD. Movable types made of baked clay were first produced around 1050 AD and there is definite evidence that metal types were already known in Korea in 1392.

Handsetting

For hundreds of years, handsetting was the only way of setting type. The method is to assemble single lead types into a line. A number of lines placed in position and provided with the required spacing material make up a

rial, ergeben die Druckform. Nach Gebrauch muss sie wieder abgelegt werden; die Buchstaben und das Blindmaterial können wieder verwendet werden.

Schon frühzeitig suchten die Buchdrucker einen möglichst günstigen Weg, um beim Setzen der Einzeltypen auf eine optimale Leistung zu kommen. Sie ordneten die Typen in wohlüberlegt eingeteilten Setzkästen in einer Weise an, die der Häufigkeit der zu brauchenden Lettern entsprach. Später ging man sogar so weit, ein Logotypensystem zu schaffen, das heisst, häufig gebrauchte Wörter und Silben zusammenzugiessen, um so das Setzen zu beschleunigen.

Typensetzmaschine

Durch Einführung der allgemeinen Schulpflicht wurde dem Analphabetentum Einhalt geboten. Das Bedürfnis nach mehr Information und somit nach mehr Gedrucktem erforderte schnellere Druckmaschinen. 1812 wurde die Schnellpresse von Friedrich König erfunden. Diese Erfindung erforderte eine rationellere Satzherstellung. Einige Jahre später wurden die ersten Patente für Setzmaschinen angemeldet. Bekannt wurde unter vielen anderen die Typensetzmaschine des Engländers Dr. William Church (1822); allerdings war bei dieser Maschine kein Ablegmechanismus vorhanden. 1870 wurde schliesslich eine brauchbare Maschine erfunden, die sogenannte Kastenbeinsche Setzmaschine. An dieser Maschine mussten vier Personen arbeiten: ein Setzer, ein Ausschliesser, ein Ableger und ein Hilfsarbeiter, der die leeren Magazine wieder mit Buchstaben nachfüllte. Diese Technik war aber nur möglich, weil Typen durch die Erfindung der Komplettgiessmaschine im Jahre 1862 in grossem Umfang hergestellt werden konnten.

printing forme. After printing, the types and spaces must be set aside for re-use.

At an early stage, printers looked for the best possible way of optimizing performance in the setting of single types. They arranged the types in cases with compartments carefully planned to suit the frequency of use of each letter. Later on they went so far as to introduce a system of logotypes, casting frequently used words and syllables in one piece, in order to speed up the setting process.

Typesetting machines

The introduction of compulsory education brought an end to general illiteracy. The need for more information in printed form brought the need for faster printing machines, and in 1812 the cylinder press was invented by Friedrich Koenig. This invention made it necessary to find a more rational way of setting type, and the first patent applications for typesetting machines were filed a few years later, among many others an invention by an Englishman, Dr William Church, in 1822, although his machine had no mechanism for "distribution", or the return of used types. A usable machine was finally invented in 1870, known as the Kastenbein typesetting machine. It required manning by four people: a typesetter, a "justifier" to equalize the line lengths, a distributor, and an assistant to refill the empty type magazines. This technique became possible only through the invention of the type-casting machine (1862), which made it possible to manufacture printing types in large quantities.

Matrizensetz- und Zeilengiessmaschinen

Abschluss dieser langen Kette von Erfindungen bildeten schliesslich die Zeilensetzmaschinen Linotype (Ottmar Mergenthaler, 1884), Typograph (John R. Rogers, 1888) und Intertype (W.S. Scudder, 1913). Sie vereinigen mechanisches Setzen von Matrizen, automatisches Ausschliessen, Giessen und Ablegen.

Durch die Tastatur werden Matrizen im Magazin ausgelöst, durch Führungsbleche zur Zeile gesammelt, mit Keilen ausgeschlossen, anschliessend gegossen und auf ein Schiff ausgestossen. Nach dem Giessen werden die Matrizen zum Ableger geführt. Durch unterschiedliche Zahnung gelenkt, fallen die Matrizen in die entsprechenden Magazinkanäle zurück.

Einzelbuchstabensetz- und -giessmaschine

1897 erfand Tolbert Lanston das Prinzip der Einzelbuchstabensetz- und -giessmaschine Monotype. Beim Einzelbuchstabensatz sind die Vorgänge «Text erfassen» und «Text ausgeben» voneinander getrennt. Der wesentliche Rationalisierungseffekt lag darin, dass die Geschwindigkeit der Giessmaschine nicht mehr von der Tastleistung des Setzers abhängig war (Giessleistung 8000 bis 12 000 Zeichen pro Stunde).

Beim Tasten wird ein 31-Kanal-Lochband gestanzt, das zur Steuerung der Giessmaschine dient. Die zum Giessen benötigten Zeichen sind in einem Matrizenrahmen nach Dickten geordnet. Dieser wird über die Öffnung der Giessform in Position gebracht, und das entsprechende Zeichen wird ausgegossen. Danach wird der Buchstabe in den Zeilenkanal gehoben und die vollständige Zeile auf ein Setzschiff geschoben.

Matrix-Setting and Line-Casting Machines

This long chain of inventions finally led to the line-casting machines: Linotype (Ottmar Mergenthaler, 1884), Typograph (John R. Rogers, 1888) and Intertype (W.S. Scudder, 1913). These combine the mechanical setting of type matrices with automatic line justification, casting and distribution.

Operation of the keyboard releases matrices from the magazine for assembly between guide rails, justification by means of double-wedge spacebands, casting and delivery of solid lines of type ("slugs") to a galley. After casting, the matrices are picked up by a mechanical arm and taken to a bar at the top of the magazine, from where they fall into the appropriate channels owing to the key-like arrangement of their teeth in different patterns.

Single-Character Setting and Casting Machine

In 1897 Tolbert Lanston invented the principle of the Monotype single-character setting and casting machine. In this process the text entry and output functions are separated. The main rationalization effect was that the speed of the casting machine was no longer dependent upon the keyboard speed of the operator, allowing casting speeds of 8,000 to 12,000 characters per hour.

The keyboard unit produces a 31-channel punched paper tape which serves to control the casting unit, where the required characters are held in the form of matrices, arranged in a case in accordance with their set-widths. The case is brought into position over the casting cavity of the composition mould and the corresponding character is cast, then lifted to the line channel, from which complete lines are ejected into a galley.

Matrizenhandsatz

Beim Matrizenhandsatz (Ludlow, 1906, und Nebitype) werden die Matrizen von Hand gesetzt, zeilenweise gegossen und wieder abgelegt. Dieses Verfahren wurde vor allem im Zeitungs- und Zeitschriftensatz für Titel und Inserate angewendet.

Mit all diesen Erfindungen war es um die Wende des 20. Jahrhunderts möglich, die Massenproduktion von Texten wirtschaftlich zu realisieren.

Teletypesettersystem (TTS)

Eine weitere Erhöhung der Ausgabeleistung wurde 1928 durch die Erfindung des TTS-Systems erreicht. Auf einem Perforator wird ein 6-Kanal-Lochstreifen gestanzt. Man unterscheidet zwischen Endlos- und ausschliessenden Perforatoren, mit oder ohne Klarschriftbeleg, mit oder ohne Display. Dieser Lochstreifen steuert die Zeilengiessmaschine. Damit konnte die Ausgabeleistung auf 30 000 Zeichen pro Stunde erhöht werden.

Der Grundgedanke des TTS-Systems war eine Fernsetzeinrichtung (Teletypesetter Corporation, Chicago). Damit war es möglich, von einer Zentralstelle aus mehrere an verschiedenen Orten stehende Setzmaschinen durch elektrische Fernsteuerung zu betätigen.

Bleisatz ist für kein Druckverfahren, ausgenommen Hochdruck, die ideale Voraussetzung. Deshalb verlor er mit dem Aufkommen des Offset- und Tiefdrucks zunehmend an Bedeutung – zugunsten des Fotosatzes.

Matrix Handsetting

In matrix handsetting (Ludlow 1906 and Nebitype), the matrices are assembled by hand, cast in lines and then distributed. This process was mainly used in setting headlines and display advertisements for newspapers and periodicals.

All these inventions made the mass production of texts economical by about the beginning of the 20th century.

Teletypesetting (TTS)

A further increase in output speed was achieved in 1928 with the invention of the TTS system. A six-channel paper tape is punched at a perforator keyboard, of which there are different kinds for "endless" and justified tape, with or without hard copy production and display panel. The paper tape runs the line-casting machine, bringing output up to a possible 30,000 characters per hour.

The basic purpose of the TTS system (Teletypesetter Corporation, Chicago) was to allow remote control of typesetting. From a central location TTS tape could be output by electrical remote control at a number of different places for the automatic operation of typesetting machines.

Metal setting is not the ideal method for any printing process other than letterpress, so its importance increasingly gave way to that of phototypesetting with the advent of offset-lithography and photogravure printing.

Vorläufer

Der Ursprung des Fotosatzes geht bis ins 19. Jahrhundert zurück. Eine der ersten Fotosetzmaschinen entwickelte der ungarische Ingenieur E. Porzsolt im Jahr 1894. Diese Maschine wurde über eine Tastatur bedient. Durch reflektiertes Licht wurden die einzelnen Buchstaben auf eine lichtempfindliche Platte fotografiert. Man erkannte schon um 1900 den Vorteil, Texte, die im Offset- oder Tiefdruck reproduziert werden sollten, direkt auf Fotomaterial zu belichten. Damit beginnt die eigentliche Geschichte des Fotosatzes.

Anfang des 20. Jahrhunderts wurden verschiedene Fotosetzmaschinen entwickelt, unter anderen die Photoline, die August-Hunter-Maschine, die Flickertype, die Orotype und die Uhertype. Die Uhertype, vom Ungaren Edmund Uher 1928 entwickelt, kam erst 1936 unter dem Namen Luminotype auf den Markt und wird heute allgemein als Vorläufer der modernen Fotosetzmaschinen angesehen. Grundsätzlich ging aber die allgemeine Entwicklung nur langsam voran. Einer der wesentlichsten Gründe lag wohl darin, dass zuerst hochwertiges Fotomaterial, welches auch zur Wiedergabe kleinster Schriftgrade geeignet ist, entwickelt werden musste. Erst nach der Lösung dieses Problems setzte die Verbreitung des Fotosatzes ein.

Mechanische Fotosetzmaschinen

In den vierziger Jahren fanden die ersten Fotosetzmaschinen Eingang in das Druckereigewerbe.

Der Fotosetter der Firma Harris-Intertype (1948) funktionierte nach dem Prinzip der Intertype-Bleisetzmaschine. An der Breitseite der Matrize ist ein Negativ-Filmbuchstabe eingebaut, an Stelle der Giessanlage tritt eine fotografische Einrichtung. Die Arbeitsgeschwindigkeit betrug 6000 bis 8000 Zei-

Forerunners

The origins of phototypesetting go back to the 19th century, one of the first photosetters having been developed by the Hungarian engineer Eugene Porzsolt in 1894. This machine was keyboard-operated and each character was photographed by reflected light on to a photosensitive plate. By 1900, the advantage of directly exposing texts destined for offset-litho or gravure printing on to photographic material had already been recognized. With this realization the history of photosetting begins.

At the beginning of the 20th century various photosetting machines were developed, among others the Photoline, the August Hunter machine, the Flickertype, the Orotype and the Uhertype. The latter, developed by the Hungarian Edmund Uher in 1928, reached the market in 1936 under the name of Luminotype, and it is now generally regarded as having been the forerunner of modern photosetting machines. Development in general was, however, rather slow. One of the main reasons for this was presumably the prior need for the introduction of high-quality photographic materials suitable for the reproduction of even the smallest type sizes. The general use of photosetting did not set in until after this problem had been solved.

Mechanical Photosetters

The first phototypesetting machines came into use in the printing trade during the 1940s.

The Harris-Intertype "Fotosetter" (1948) operated on the same principle as the Intertype linecaster. The matrices have negative film letters in place of punched letters and a camera takes the place of the casting mechanism. Working speed was about 6,000 to 8,000 characters per hour. The Fotosetter

chen pro Stunde. Der Fotosetter war die erste praktisch und wirtschaftlich erfolgreich arbeitende Fotosetzmaschine.

Auch für den Titel- und Akzidenzsatz waren bald praxisreife Geräte auf dem Markt. Von Perry wurde das Fotosetzgerät Headliner konstruiert, welches nur für den Satz von Titelzeilen verwendbar war. Vom Holländer de Goeij wurde das erste Akzidenz-Fotosetzgerät «Hadego» entwickelt. Es wurde 1948 in Betrieb genommen und arbeitete mit Kunststofflettern, die einzeln zusammengesetzt und dann zeilenweise fotografiert wurden.

Eine weitere erfolgreiche Maschine, die Monophoto, wurde um 1957 von der Monotype Corporation herausgebracht. Das System dieser Maschine basiert ebenfalls auf den Schriftguss-Monotype-Maschinen. Sie besteht aus einer Tasteinheit und einer Belichtungsmaschine. Der 31-Kanal-Lochstreifen steuert den Negativfilm-Matrizenrahmen. Belichtungsleistung rund 10 000 Zeichen pro Stunde.

Elektromechanische Fotosetzmaschinen

Die französischen Ingenieure Higonnet und Moyroud hatten die Idee, als Negativmatrizen runde Schriftscheiben zu verwenden. Das Modell ihrer Fotosetzmaschine wurde in Amerika vollendet und erschien zuerst unter dem Namen Lumitype auf dem Markt. Später wurden diese Maschinen unter dem Namen Photon (1956 in Europa) bekannt. Die Hauptbestandteile sind eine Tasteinheit mit Schreibmaschinentastatur, ein Telefonrelaissystem und eine fotografische Belichtungseinheit. Die gesetzten Buchstaben werden bis zur vollständigen Zeile im Relaissystem gespeichert, die Zeilenendtaste gibt den Befehl zum Ausschliessen. Mit der Erfassung entsteht gleichzeitig eine Schreibmaschinenklarschrift für Korrekturzwecke. Die Belichtung erfolgt durch eine rotierende

was the first practical and economically successful phototypesetter.

Practical machines for photosetting headlines and jobbing work were also introduced during the same period. The "Headliner", suitable only for display setting, was made by Perry. The first jobbing photosetter, the "Hadego" was developed by the Dutchman de Goeij. Launched in 1948, it operated with plastic letters which were assembled individually and photographed line by line.

Another successful machine, the "Monophoto", was introduced by the Monotype Corporation in 1957. Its operation is similarly based on that of Monotype hot-metal typecasting. It consists of a keyboard unit and a photo unit. The 31-channel perforated tape controls the negative film matrix case, at an exposure speed of about 10,000 cph.

Electromechanical Photosetters

The French engineers Higonnet and Moyroud had the idea of using circular type discs as negative matrices. Their model of photosetter was brought into production in America and was first introduced under the name of the "Lumitype", later becoming known as the "Photon" and available in Europe from 1956. Its main components are a keyboard unit with typewriter layout, a telephone relay system and a photographic exposure unit. The characters keyboarded are stored in the relay system until the line is complete, when the "line-ending" key is used for justification. Copy entry simultaneously produces typewritten hard copy for proofreading. Exposure is by means of a rotating negative type disc, at a speed of around 30,000 characters per hour.

Negativschriftscheibe mit einer Geschwindigkeit von rund 30 000 Zeichen pro Stunde.

Ab Mitte des 20. Jahrhunderts wurde eine grosse Anzahl von Fotosetzgeräten und Fotosetzmaschinen auf den Markt gebracht. Waren anfangs nur geringe Belichtungsleistungen möglich, erfuhr die Entwicklung bald eine Steigerung bis zu mehreren hunderttausend Buchstaben pro Stunde.

Einen grossen Erfolg hatte die Firma Berthold, Berlin, mit dem Akzidenzgerät Diatype (1962) und 1968 mit der Diatronic-Fotosetzmaschine.

In diesem Zeitraum kamen auch eine Vielzahl von Titelsetzgeräten auf den Markt. Sie arbeiten nach dem Vergrösserungsprinzip und/oder besitzen ein Zoomobjektiv, zum Beispiel Staromat, Typomatik usw.

Elektronische Fotosetzanlagen

Eine entscheidende Erfindung war die elektronische Arbeitsweise mit digitalisierten Schriften von Dr. Hell, Kiel (1966). Die Digiset-Lichtsetzanlage arbeitet mit einer Kathodenstrahlröhre und löst die Schrift in einzelne Punkte auf, die beim Belichtungsvorgang aus dem Kernspeicher abgerufen und auf das fotografische Material aufgezeichnet werden (Belichtungsgeschwindigkeit je nach Auflösung 1 bis 2 Millionen Zeichen pro Stunde).

Eine andere Belichtungsart hat das Linotron-Modell von 1967. Es arbeitet ebenfalls mit Kathodenstrahl, doch ist ein reales Schriftbild vorhanden, welches durch eine Röhre in einzelne Linien aufgelöst und mit einer zweiten aufgezeichnet wird. Die Belichtungsleistung beträgt je nach Auflösungsstufe rund 450 000 Zeichen pro Stunde.

After 1950 a large number of text and display photosetters were brought onto the market. Although the exposure speeds were at first slow, further development soon brought increasing rates, up to several hundred thousand characters per hour.
The firm of Berthold, based in Berlin, had great success with the Diatype jobbing photosetter (1962), followed in 1968 by the Diatronic machine.

During the same period, a large number of photo-headliners were also introduced. Working on the enlargement principle and/or possessing a zoom lens, they included the Staromat, Typomatic machines, etc.

Electronic Photosetters

A decisive invention made by the Dr Hell company of Kiel in 1966 was electronic operation with digitized types. The Digiset photosetter uses a cathode-ray tube for exposure and resolves the type into dots, which are called up from the core store during the exposure process and recorded on the photographic material at a speed of 1 to 2 million cph, depending on the fineness of resolution.

A different method of exposure was used by the first Linotron of 1967. It also uses a CRT but has real-type images, which are resolved into lines by one light-tube and recorded by another. Depending on resolution, the speed of exposure is around 450,000 cph.

Weiterentwicklung

Die Tendenz ab 1972 sind Neuerscheinungen von Belichtungsanlagen mit mittleren Geschwindigkeiten. Viele Belichter verfügen über einen integrierten Satzrechner und ermöglichen die Verarbeitung von Endlosdatenträgern. Mit der Linotronic (1976) erhält die Diatronic eine echte Konkurrenz. Mit diesen und mit anderen Maschinen wird auch den Druckereien mit geringem Satzaufkommen der Weg zum Fotosatz geebnet.

Für die Grossdruckereien, hauptsächlich Zeitungsbetriebe, bieten die Lieferfirmen die sogenannten integrierten Satzsysteme an (GSA 780, Harris 2500, Hell/Siemens Cosy, Linotype System 5 usw.). Es handelt sich um komplette Textverarbeitungssysteme aus Hard- und Softwarebausteinen zur automatischen Satzproduktion.

Im Akzidenzbereich führt der Weg seit 1978 weg von der Direkteingabe. Die Geräte sind mit Bildschirmen versehen, arbeiten mit Datensicherung (Floppy Disk) und Datenträgersteuerung. Kompaktsysteme können durch weitere Erfassungsplätze zu kleinen Verbundsystemen ausgebaut werden (Linotronic, Compugraphic cg 7500, Eurocat 150, Berthold ACS, CRTronic usw.). Bei Klein- und Grosssystemen können Darstellungsbildschirme angeschlossen werden. Sie dienen zur optischen Kontrolle vor der Belichtung.

1977 kam der erste Laserbelichter Lasercomp von Monotype auf den Markt. Im Unterschied zur CRT-Belichtung erfolgt die Aufzeichnung meistens horizontal. Heute ist die Laseraufzeichnung für Raster die ideale Voraussetzung.

Die Möglichkeiten des Ganzseitenumbruchs am Bildschirm und die Ganzseitenbelichtung, einschliesslich Schwarzweiss-Rasterbildern, werden laufend optimiert. Interaktive Workstations und Desktop-Publishing erobern den Markt.

Further Development

Since 1972 the trend has been towards new kinds of photo units with medium speeds. Many of these units have an integrated typesetting computer, allowing the acceptance of "endless" data carriers. By 1976, the Linotronic and the Diatronic were in competition and with these and other machines the road to photosetting was opened even for companies with limited typesetting requirements.

For large-scale printing operations, particularly in the newspaper world, the suppliers offer integrated typesetting systems such as the GSA 780, Harris 2500, Hell/Siemens Cosy, Linotype System 5, etc. These are complete text-processing systems comprising hardware and software modules for automatic typesetting.

In the general printing field, the trend since 1978 has been away from direct entry. Units are equipped with display screens and operate with data protection (floppy discs) and data-carrier control. Compact systems (Linotronic, Compugraphic cg 7500, Eurocat 150, Berthold ACS, CRTronic, etc.) can be extended to make small grouped systems by the addition of extra entry stations.

Visual display terminals for the optical control of exposure can be connected to both large and small systems.

In 1977, Monotype introduced the first laser exposure system, "Lasercomp". Unlike CRT exposure, laser exposure is usually horizontal. Today, laser recording is the ideal method for raster image processing.

Constant improvement is being made to the methods of full-page make-up on screen and full-page exposure, including monochrome halftones, while interactive workstations and desktop publishing systems are having a profound effect on the market.

Die nachfolgend aufgeführten Verfahren sind für die professionelle Satzherstellung ungeeignet. Sie werden vor allem für die Herstellung von Drucksachen angewendet, die keine hohen Qualitätsansprüche stellen und deshalb teure Satzkosten nicht rechtfertigen.

The methods described in this section are not suitable for professional standards of typesetting. They are mainly used for the production of printed matter which does not have any high quality requirements and therefore does not justify high setting costs.

Schreibsatz

Der Schreibsatz verbreitete sich parallel zur Entwicklung des Kleinoffsetdrucks, um die Satzkosten für Drucksachen mit geringer Auflage möglichst niedrig zu halten. Die technische Entwicklung des Schreibsatzes geht zum Teil von der Schreibmaschine aus.

Typewriter Setting

Typewriter or "strike-on" setting developed in parallel with small-offset printing in order to keep the setting costs for short-run work as low as possible. The technical development of "strike-on" setting is based to some extent on the ordinary office typewriter.

Schreibmaschinen
Jede Schreibmaschine kann zur Textvorlagenherstellung benutzt werden. Das Schriftbild ist jedoch unausgeglichen (alle Zeichen haben die gleiche Breite), und es kann nur linksbündiger Flattersatz getippt werden.

Typewriters
Any typewriter can be used for the production of text originals, but the appearance of the matter is unbalanced (each character having the same width) and all text must be unjustified (flush left and ragged right).

Schreibsetzmaschinen
Mit einer speziellen Schreibmaschine werden kopierfähige Spezialpapiere und -filme beschrieben. Ein auswechselbarer Schreibkopf ermöglicht die Darstellung unterschiedlicher Schriften und Schriftgrössen. Es wurde versucht, die Druckschriften zu kopieren sowie typografische Gestaltungsformen zu ermöglichen.
Anfänglich war für Blocksatz eine zweite Niederschrift notwendig (IBM-Composer 72). Eine Weiterentwicklung ist der IBM-Composer 82. Dieser verfügt über einen Arbeitsspeicher und kann Zeilen automatisch ausschliessen. Beim IBM-MC-Composer werden Texte und Anweisungen auf Magnetkarten gespeichert und können sofort oder nachträglich ausgegeben werden. Die gespeicherten Informationen können beliebig korrigiert, überarbeitet und umbrochen werden.

Typewriter Setting Machines
Photographic papers and films can be used with special "strike-on" machines. An exchangeable type head allows the production of different typefaces and sizes and a serious attempt was made to copy printers' typefaces and provide facilities for typographical design.
At first a second keyboarding was required for justified setting (IBM Composer 72). A further development, the IBM Composer 82, has a computer memory and can therefore justify lines automatically.
With the IBM-MC Composer, texts and instructions are stored on magnetic cards for immediate or subsequent output. The stored information can be corrected, edited and divided at will.

Textsysteme, Personalcomputer (PC)
Alle Textsysteme und PCs können zur Vorlagenherstellung von Texten und Tabellen

Text Systems, Personal Computers (PC)
All text systems and PCs can be used for the production of texts and tables for reproduction. These units have computer storage and data carriers, allowing texts to be altered and

eingesetzt werden. Sie verfügen über einen Arbeitsspeicher sowie Datenträger. Die Texte können beliebig verändert und umgestaltet werden. Diese Geräte ermöglichen auch gewisse typografische Gestaltungsformen und Satzarten wie Blocksatz, Flattersatz sowie das Ziehen von waagrechten und senkrechten Linien. Die Reproduktionsfähigkeit der Vorlage ist abhängig von der Qualität der Druckerausgabe.

Desktop-Publishing
Desktop-Publishing ist eine Weiterentwicklung der «Schreibmaschinenkultur» und entwickelte sich praktisch und historisch völlig unabhängig von den Satzprogrammen und der Belichtertechnologie.
Vieles, was früher mit der Schreibmaschine nur sehr ungenügend gestaltet werden konnte, ist nun sehr preiswert und besser zu realisieren.
Die Grenze zwischen Satz und Desktop-Publishing-Verfahren ist nicht technischer Natur, sondern abhängig vom typografischen und «handwerklichen» Können des Bedieners.

Andere Verfahren

Abreibschriften
Sie werden vor allem für Entwürfe und Beschriftungen angewendet.
Ein Vorteil dieses Verfahrens liegt darin, dass neben Schriften in vielen Grössen und Arten auch Signete, Umrandungen, Raster und typografischer Schmuck lieferbar sind (zum Beispiel Letraset, Mecanorma).

Handschriftliche Vorlagen
Von Hand geschriebene, gemalte, gezeichnete oder gespritzte Vorlagen sind im weitesten Sinne auch als eine Art von Satzherstellung zu betrachten. Im weiteren gehören auch die Stempelschriften zu den sogenannten anderen Verfahren.

rearranged at will. These features, together with justified setting and other variations such as centred and flush right unjustified matter and the drawing of horizontal and vertical rules, provide a certain measure of typographical resource for design purposes. Here the reproduction quality of the copy is dependent upon the nature of the print-out device.

Desktop Publishing
Desktop publishing is a further development of the "typewriter culture" and has developed quite independently of typesetting software and exposure technology, in both practical and historical terms. Many kinds of work which could formerly be produced only in an aesthetically inferior form on the typewriter can now be "better" designed at low cost. The boundary between the typesetting and desktop publishing processes is not of a technical nature but depends on the typographic knowledge and craft skill of the user.

Other Methods

Dry-Transfer Lettering
Dry-transfer letters are mainly used for preliminary designs and lettering work. An advantage of the method is that, in addition to typefaces in many sizes and styles, the suppliers (e.g. Letraset, Mecanorma) can provide signs and symbols, borders, tints, vignettes, and typographical ornaments.

Handwritten Copy
Handwritten copy in a suitable form for reproduction can also be regarded as a kind of typesetting in the widest sense. Stamped characters also belong to our category of "other methods".

Systematik Fotosatz

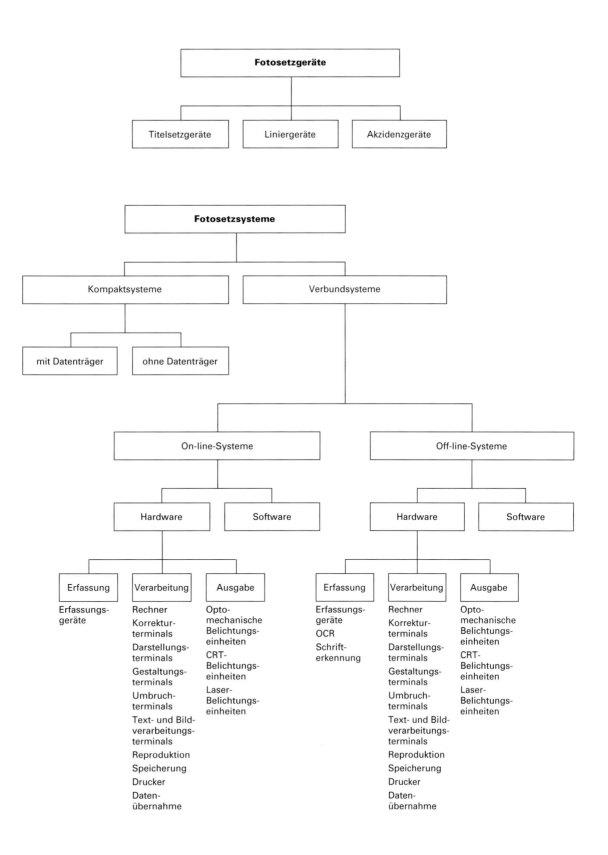

Phototypesetting Logistics

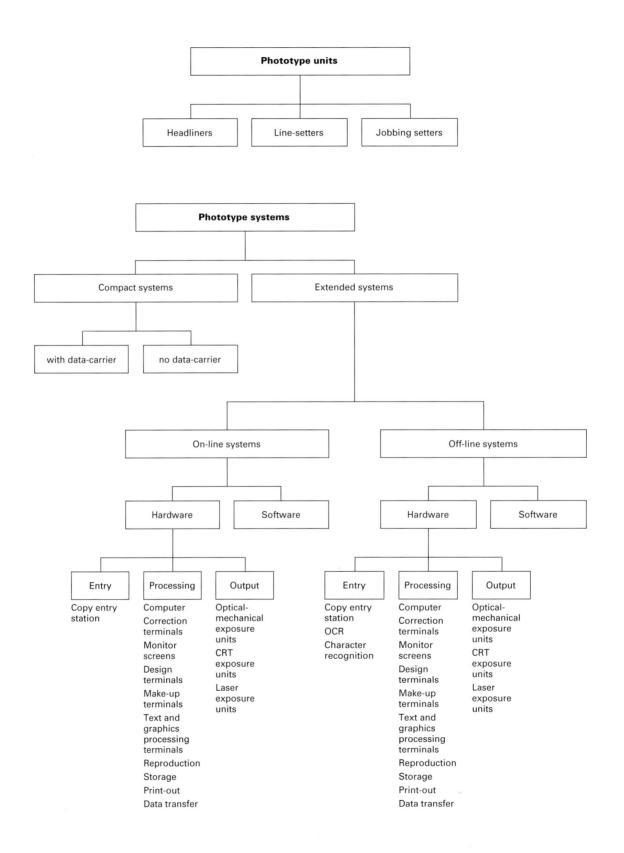

Fotosetzgeräte haben keinen automatischen Zeilenausschluss, so dass Blocksatz oder Satz auf Mittelachse nur durch zweimaliges Setzen hergestellt werden können. Die Fotosetzgeräte sind gegliedert in Titelsetzgeräte, Akzidenzgeräte und Liniergeräte, wovon die beiden letztgenannten fast ausnahmslos aus der Praxis verschwunden sind.

This category covers photosetting machines without any automatic justification of lines. With these machines, the setting operation has to be carried out twice if justification or centring of copy is required. In addition to headliners and jobbing setters there are rule-setting devices, but the last two kinds have almost entirely gone out of use today.

Titelsetzgeräte

Diese Geräte werden vorwiegend für einzelne Wörter und Zeilen in grösseren Graden eingesetzt. Der Schriftgrössenbereich ist abhängig vom Prinzip der einzelnen Geräte.

Geräte auf Kontaktbasis
Die Belichtung erfolgt im Kontakt 1:1. Der Schriftgrössenbereich ist abhängig von der Schriftgrösse des Originals (zum Beispiel Optiset, Strip-Printer).

Geräte auf Vergrösserungsbasis
Bei diesen Geräten kann die Schrift vom gleichen Schriftbildträger durch Verschieben des Projektionskopfes vergrössert oder verkleinert werden (zum Beispiel Staromat, Letterphot).

Geräte mit Vergrösserungsoptik
Auch bei diesen Geräten kann die Schriftgrösse vom gleichen Schriftbildträger verändert werden. Die Vergrösserung der Zeichen erfolgt mit einem Zoomobjektiv (Vergrösserungsoptik); der Projektionskopf ist fest (zum Beispiel Typomatik).

Bei einigen Titelsetzgeräten kann die Bedienung über eine Buchstabenauswählvorrichtung (zum Beispiel Diatype-Headliner) oder durch die Steuerung einer Tastatur erfolgen (zum Beispiel Compugraphic cg 7200).

Display Photosetters

These devices, also known as headliners, are mainly used for setting single words and lines in the larger type sizes. The range of sizes available depends on the operating pinciple of the machine concerned.

Contact Models
Exposure is by photographic contact in same size, 1:1, so the size range is dependent upon the originals (e.g. Optiset, Strip-Printer).

Enlarging Models
With these, the original type image can be enlarged or reduced by moving the projection head (e.g. Staromat, Letterphot).

Optical Enlarging Models
These also provide for the scaling of the original, but enlargement is obtained with a zoom lens (enlargement optics) and the projection head is fixed (e.g. Typomatik).

Some of these photosetters have a device for selection of characters (e.g. Diatype Headliner) or control by keyboard (e.g. Compugraphic cg 7200).

Akzidenzgeräte

Mit den Akzidenzgeräten ist standrichtiges Setzen, einschliesslich Linienbelichtung, auf Blattfilm möglich. Die Buchstaben werden einzeln auf Fotopapier oder Film belichtet. Der Dicktentransport erfolgt automatisch. Die Geräte besitzen keine Korrekturmöglichkeit. Für Mengensatz sind sie nicht geeignet, weil sie keinen automatischen Zeilenausschluss ausführen können (zum Beispiel Diatype).

Jobbing Photosetters

With jobbing machines, regular typesetting including line exposure on sheet film was possible. Characters were exposed one at a time on photographic paper or film, with automatic transport for the required set-width. They had no method of correction and were unsuitable for setting long texts because they had no means of automatic justification (e.g. Diatype).

Liniergeräte

Diese Geräte werden ausschliesslich für den Liniensatz eingesetzt (Tabellen, Formulare); es können keine Texte gesetzt werden (zum Beispiel Dialiner, Fotoliner).

Rule Setters

These were used exclusively for setting rules for tables and forms and had no facilities for text setting (e.g. Dialiner, Fotoliner).

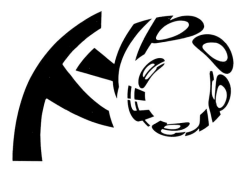

Fototechnische Satzmöglichkeiten mit verschiedenen Geräten. Phototechnical possibilities of typesetting, using various machines.

Fotosetzsysteme   **Photosetting Systems**

Fotosetzsysteme können mit Hilfe eines Rechners Zeilen automatisch (elektronisch) ausschliessen, die Dicktenwerte werden gezählt. Alle modernen Fotosetzsysteme verfügen zudem über die Möglichkeit der Datenspeicherung. Es wird zwischen *Kompaktsystemen* (Einplatzsystemen) und *Verbundsystemen* (Mehrplatzsystemen) unterschieden.

Photosetting systems are able to justify lines automatically (electronically) by means of a computer, with counting of all character widths. All modern systems also have the facility of data storage. A distinction has to be made between *compact systems* with only one workstation and *grouped systems* with more than one.

Kompaktsysteme

Compact Systems

Merkmal der Kompaktsysteme ist, dass Erfassung, Verarbeitung und Ausgabe in ein System integriert sind, das heisst entweder in einem gemeinsamen Gehäuse oder durch eine starre Verbindung zusammengeschlossen. Jede der drei Prozessstufen ist dabei nur einfach ausgelegt. Sobald dieses Verhältnis geändert wird, zum Beispiel durch Erweiterung um einen zweiten Erfassungsplatz, wird das Kompaktsystem bereits zu einem kleinen Verbundsystem.

These are characterized by the integration of copy entry, processing and output in a single system, whether it is housed in a single unit or formed by a fixed connection of units. In such a system, each of the three stages of the photosetting process is in single form. As soon as this one-to-one ratio is changed, e.g. by the addition of a second copy entry station, the compact system has already become a small grouped system.

Kompaktsysteme ohne Datenträger

Compact Systems without Data Carrier

Diese Systeme sind weitgehend von der technischen Entwicklung überholt, da sie wegen der fehlenden Möglichkeit der Datenspeicherung erheblichen Arbeitsaufwand verursachen (zum Beispiel bei Korrekturen); zudem können sie nicht zu Verbundsystemen ausgebaut werden (zum Beispiel Diatronic, Linocomp).

These systems have been largely overtaken by technical progress, since their lack of data storage facilities gives rise to a considerable expenditure of labour, for example in making corrections. Moreover, they are not capable of being extended to make grouped systems (e.g. Diatronic, Linocomp).

Kompaktsysteme mit Datenträger

Compact Systems with Data Carrier

Ohne Simultanbetrieb
Bei diesen Systemen kann jeweils nur eine Arbeit ausgeführt werden. Es ist nicht möglich, einen Text zu erfassen oder zu korrigieren und gleichzeitig einen anderen zu belichten (zum Beispiel Linotronic I, Compugraphic cg 7500).

Without Multi-Tasking
Only one task at a time can be carried out on these systems. It is not possible to enter or correct a text while at the same time exposing another one (e.g. Linotronic I, Compugraphic cg 7500).

Mit Simultanbetrieb
Diese Kompaktsysteme bieten die Möglichkeit, Vordergrund (Erfassung) und Hintergrund (Belichter) unabhängig voneinander zu betreiben. Es kann so gleichzeitig (simultan) Auftrag A erfasst oder korrigiert und Auftrag B belichtet werden (zum Beispiel Berthold ACS, Linotype CRTronic).

Verbundsysteme

Bei den Verbundsystemen wird nach der Systemarchitektur unterschieden in *On-line-Systeme* und *Off-line-Systeme*. Beide Gruppen bestehen jeweils aus *Hardware* und *Software*. Die Hardware ist nochmals untergliedert in Geräte und Maschinen zur *Erfassung, Verarbeitung* und *Ausgabe*.

On-line-Systeme

On line heisst: in direkter Verbindung mit der Datenverarbeitungsanlage arbeitend. Beim On-line-Betrieb können mehrere Erfassungsplätze direkt an die Verarbeitung (Rechner) und an den Belichter angeschlossen werden.

Off-line-Systeme

Off line heisst: getrennt von der Datenverarbeitungsanlage arbeitend. Die Erfassungsplätze sind mit eigenen Datenträgern ausgerüstet; die erfassten Texte werden zuerst auf diesen zwischengespeichert. Anschliessend werden sie an die Zentraleinheit (Rechner) zur Verarbeitung und nachher zur Belichtungseinheit (Ausgabe) weitergegeben.

Hardware

Unter Hardware versteht man die materiellen Bestandteile (Maschinen und Geräte) einer EDV-Anlage.

With Multi-Tasking
These compact systems offer the possibility of carrying out foreground (entry) and background (e.g. exposure) work independently of one another, so that job A can be entered or corrected at the same time as job B is being exposed (e.g. Berthold ACS, Linotype CRTronic).

Grouped Systems

Grouped systems are classified in accordance with their system architecture as *on-line* or *off-line systems,* both kinds comprising *hardware* and *software*. The hardware is further divided into equipment and machinery for *copy entry, processing* and *output*.

On-line Systems

The term "on-line" means operating in direct connection with the data processing equipment. In on-line systems, several entry stations can be connected directly to the processor (computer) and the exposure (photo unit).

Off-line Systems

The term "off-line" means operating separately from the data processing equipment. The entry stations are each equipped with their own data carriers, where the input texts are at first held in store. Subsequently they are passed on to the central processing unit and to the exposure unit for output.

Hardware

The term "hardware" means the material components (machinery and equipment) of a data processing installation.

Software

Unter Software versteht man die immateriellen Bestandteile einer EDV-Anlage, also die Gesamtheit der Programme. Man unterscheidet zwei Arten von Programmen: Programme des Betriebssystems und Anwender- oder Benutzerprogramme. Ein Programm bewirkt die automatische Ausführung einer Aufgabe (zum Beispiel Silbentrennung). Es besteht aus einer geordneten Folge von Instruktionen für den Rechner und kann beliebig oft für dieselbe Aufgabe mit verschiedenen Daten benutzt werden. Je nach Art der Aufgabenstellung bieten die Fotosatzhersteller für verschiedene Satzbereiche Programme an, zum Beispiel Silbentrennprogramme, Umbruchprogramme, Ästhetikprogramme usw.

Software

The term "software" means the nonmaterial components of a data processing installation, i.e. the totality of the programming. A distinction is made between two types of programs, those of the operating system and those which are applied by the user. A program puts into effect the automatic functioning of a task, e.g. hyphenation. It consists of an ordered sequence of instructions for the computer and can be used at will for carrying out the same task with different data. Depending on the user's order structure, phototype equipment manufacturers offer different kinds of typesetting programs, e.g. for hyphenation, make-up or typographic refinements (aesthetic programs).

Erfassung

Unter Erfassung ist in der Satzherstellung die Texterfassung gemeint. Man versteht darunter das Umsetzen eines Manuskriptes in eine für den Satzrechner verständliche Sprache. Ein Satzrechner versteht Schriftzeichen nur als Code verschlüsselt. Es wird zwischen ausschliessender (interaktiver) Texterfassung, Trennfugenbetrieb und Endloserfassung unterschieden. Je nach Systemkonfiguration kann die Texterfassung off line oder on line erfolgen.

Copy Entry

In typesetting, terms such as "entry", "input" and "data capture" are used to mean the entry of texts, i.e. the conversion of a manuscript into a language understood by the computer, which accepts typographic characters only in the form of codes. Copy entry may be in one of three forms: justifying (interactive), word-breaking or endless. Depending on the system configuration entry may be on-line or off-line.

Ausschliessende Texterfassung

Bei der ausschliessenden Texterfassung gestaltet der Bediener das Zeilenende jeweils individuell nach lesetechnischen und ästhetischen Kriterien (man wird also beispielsweise Musik-automaten und nicht Musikautomaten trennen). Ausschliessen durch den Bediener ist dann erforderlich, wenn an das Satzprodukt hohe Qualitätsansprüche gestellt werden. Der Zeitaufwand für ausschliessende Texterfassung ist gegenüber

Justifying Copy Entry

With interactive justification, the operator determines the ending of each line, in accordance with house style and lexical rules. (For example, the word musician would be hyphenated as musi-cian, not music-ian.) Hyphenation by the operator is required when the product must be of high quality, or when the equipment in use has no hyphenation program. The time required for this interactive operation is considerably greater

Endlostexterfassung um einiges grösser (abhängig von der Zeilenbreite).

Trennfugenbetrieb

Im Trennfugenbetrieb erfasst der Bediener den Text, ohne das Zeilenende zu berücksichtigen. Der Rechner beendet selbständig die Zeile vor dem letzten Wort, das nicht mehr in der festgelegten Zeilenbreite unterzubringen ist. Dabei wird der letzte Wortzwischenraum in ein Zeilenendkommando umgewandelt und der Rest des bereits erfassten Textes in die neue Zeile übernommen. Kommt aber ein langes, trennfähiges Wort in den Zeilenendbereich, so tastet der Bediener an allen Stellen, an denen sinnvoll getrennt werden kann, eine sogenannte Trennfuge (zum Beispiel Trenn-fugen-betrieb). Durch den Rechner wird ermittelt, welche Trennfuge im vorgegebenen Zeilenformat noch Platz hat. Er wandelt diese in einen Bindestrich (Divis) um, beendet die Zeile und übernimmt den Rest des getrennten Wortes in die nächste Zeile. Die nicht benötigten Trennfugen werden automatisch unterdrückt.

Endlostexterfassung

Bei der Endlostexterfassung entfallen alle Entscheidungsprobleme am Zeilenende. Der Rechner mit dem Ausschliess- und Trennprogramm bestimmt bei allen Satzarten automatisch das Zeilenende und die erforderlichen Worttrennungen. Von allen Erfassungsarten ermöglicht die Endloserfassung die höchste Erfassungsleistung. Allerdings steht dem ein eindeutiger Qualitätsabfall aufgrund der Schwächen des Ausschliess- und Silbentrennprogramms entgegen. Ausserdem ist in der Regel mit einem höheren Korrekturanteil durch Trennfehler zu rechnen.

than that for endless text entry, depending on the line length.

Operator's Word Breaks

In word-breaking operation, the operator enters the text without taking account of line endings. The computer ends the line by its own calculation before the last word which will no longer fit into the given line length. This means that the last word space in the line is converted into a line ending command and the rest of the text already entered is incorporated into the next line. However, if a long, breakable word comes into the line ending area, the operator keys in a "wordbreak" code at all the places where such a break can reasonably be made (e.g. pos-si-bil-i-ty). The computer indicates which word-break can be accommodated into the given line length, converting it into a hyphen to end the justified line and taking over the rest of the broken word into the next line. The word-breaks not required are automatically suppressed.

Endless Copy Entry

In endless copy entry there are no decisions to be made by the operator at line endings. The computer, equipped with a hyphenation and justification (H&J) program, automatically determines the line ending and the necessary word-breaks in all categories of setting. This method provides for the highest entry performance of all, although it has the disadvantage of a certain lowering of quality owing to the limitations of the H&J program, and as a general rule it involves a greater amount of correction work as a result of unacceptable word-breaks.

Off-line-Texterfassung

Beim Schreiben entsteht ein Datenträger, der anschliessend dem Satzrechner über entsprechende Eingabegeräte zur Verarbeitung eingegeben wird.

On-line-Texterfassung

Bei der On-line-Texterfassung wird der geschriebene Text über eine Leitung direkt dem Satzrechner übergeben. Der grosse Vorteil dieser Erfassungsart liegt erstens darin, dass Texte nicht nur gesendet, sondern auch wieder geholt werden können, und zweitens, dass der Ort der Texterfassung nicht mit dem Ort der Textverarbeitung übereinstimmen muss (Datenfernverarbeitung).

Wichtigstes Gerät zur On-line-Texterfassung ist der Bildschirm (Datensichtgerät). Er ermöglicht den Dialog mit dem Satzsystem. Als zusätzliche (billige) Erfassungsplätze werden auch Tastgeräte mit Display und/oder PCs eingesetzt.

Lesemaschinen (OCR)

Ein alternatives Verfahren der Texterfassung ergibt sich durch den Einsatz der Lesemaschine oder auch OCR-Belegleser genannt. (OCR ist die Abkürzung von Optical Character Recognition und heisst optische Zeichenerkennung.) Bei diesem Verfahren wird ein Klarschriftbeleg (Typoskript) als Datenträger benützt.

Eine Lesemaschine besteht aus drei Einheiten: dem Transportsystem, einer Lese- und einer Erkennungseinheit.

Off-line Copy Entry

Here keyboarding produces a data carrier which is subsequently input to the typesetting computer by means of an appropriate input device.

On-line Copy Entry

With on-line copy entry, the keyboarded text is transmitted directly to the computer through a lead. The great advantages of this method are that the text can be recalled as well as transmitted and that the keyboarding location does not have to be the same as the copy processing location (use of data transmission techniques).

The most important piece of equipment for on-line copy entry is the screen (visual display unit), which enables dialogue to take place with the typesetting system. As additional (economical) entry stations, keyboard units with small display panels and/or personal computers may be used.

Reading Machines (OCR)

An alternative method of copy entry is provided by the use of a reading machine or OCR (Optical Character Recognition) document reader. For this method a hard copy document (typescript) is used as the data carrier.

A reading machine consists of three units: the transport system, a reading unit and a recognition unit.

Arbeitsablauf

1. Endlostexterfassung mit allen typografischen Befehlen und Sonderzeichen auf einer Schreibmaschine.
2. Korrekturlesen des entstandenen Klarschriftbelegs durch den Korrektor.
3. Ausführen der Korrekturen an der Schreibmaschine.
4. Lesen des Belegs durch die Lesemaschine.
5. Übergabe des gelesenen Textes von der Lesemaschine an den Satzrechner.

Schrifterkennung

Schrifterkennung ist eine weitere alternative Methode der Texterfassung. Allerdings steht dieses Verfahren (bei Herausgabe dieses Buches) noch am Anfang der Entwicklung. Man versteht darunter im weitesten Sinn die Umwandlung von Text in eine Vektorform. Ein solches Programm ist fähig, Dokumente mit Symbolen, Kolonnen, proportionalen Schriften sowie einen bunt gemischten Inhalt von Text und Grafik zu verarbeiten. Die erstellten Textfiles lassen sich mit üblichen Textverarbeitungsprogrammen, mit Desktop-Publishing-Software oder mit Datenbanksystemen weiterverarbeiten. Es können beispielsweise automatische Silbentrennungen und Wortkorrekturen vorgenommen, der Text kann nach bestimmten Kriterien sortiert oder es kann nach Wortkombinationen gesucht werden. Weiter kann dem Text eine beliebige Schriftart und Schriftgrösse zugeordnet werden. Mit der Schrifterkennung kann man Texte aus Büchern, Zeitungen, Zeitschriften, Geschäftsbriefen, Typoskripten und von anderen Vorlagen umwandeln. Auf diese Weise können herkömmliche Abschreibarbeiten umgangen werden.

Working Procedure

1. Typewriting of endless text with all typographical commands and special signs.
2. Proofreading of the resulting hard copy.
3. Correction by typewriter.
4. Reading by the OCR machine.
5. Transmission of the copy read from the OCR machine to the typesetting computer.

Character Recognition

Character recognition is another alternative method of copy entry. It must be said that at the time of writing the method is still in the early stages of its development. In the broadest sense, OCR means the conversion of texts into a vector form. Such a program is capable of processing documents containing symbols, columns, proportional typefaces and a mixture of text and graphics. The text files produced can be further processed with the usual typesetting programs, with desktop publishing software or with data-bank systems. For example, automatic H&J and corrections are possible, the text can be sorted in accordance with given criteria or searched in accordance with combinations of words. In addition, any required typeface and size can be allocated to the text. Character recognition allows texts from books, newspapers, magazines, business letters, typescripts, and other forms of originals to be converted for data processing, eliminating the usual re-keyboarding work.

Verarbeitung

In der Satzherstellung ist der Begriff Verarbeitung (Daten- oder Textverarbeitung) so zu verstehen, dass darunter alles subsumiert wird, was weder zur Erfassung noch zur Ausgabe gehört, also nicht nur die computermässige Verarbeitung des Textes durch Ausschliessen und Silbentrennung, sondern auch der gesamte Bereich Korrektur, Gestaltung und Speicherung, inklusive der hierfür erforderlichen Zwischenausgaben (periphere Geräte).

Processing

In typesetting, the concept of data processing or copy processing is to be understood to comprise everything that comes between entry and output, i.e. not only the computerized processing of the text by hyphenation and justification but also the entire area of correction, make-up and storage, including the necessary intermediate output through peripheral equipment.

Rechner

Bei den Fotosetzsystemen (automatisierte Satzherstellung) werden für die Verarbeitung in erster Linie Satzrechner eingesetzt. Grossrechneranlagen, die neben satztechnischen Aufgaben auch für kommerzielle EDV zur Verfügung stehen, nennt man Universalrechner.

Computers

In the production of typesetting by photosetting systems, processing is done mainly by special typesetting computers. Large computer installations which are available for commercial electronic data processing in addition to typesetting tasks are known as universal or mainframe computers.

Korrekturterminals

Für die Korrektur werden meistens die gleichen Bildschirmgeräte verwendet, welche auch in der Texterfassung eingesetzt werden.

Correction Terminals

For correction, the same visual display terminals which are also used for copy entry are usually suitable.

Darstellungsterminals

Die Darstellungsbildschirme dienen zur optischen Kontrolle des Satzes. Sie verfügen über keinen eigenen Rechner. Die Sichtbarmachung kann je nach Software in Umrissdarstellung, mit symbolischer Schriftwiedergabe oder in Echttypografie erfolgen. Der Text kann am Darstellungsbildschirm nicht korrigiert werden. Bei jeder Änderung, die über das Erfassungsgerät erfolgen muss, werden einzelne Blöcke oder die ganze Arbeit neu aufgebaut.

Monitor Screens

Monitor screens serve for the visual checking of the setting. They do not have on-board computers. Depending on the software, the display can either be in outline, with "generic" typefaces or with true typefaces. The text cannot be corrected on the monitor screen. Every time an alteration is made via the copy entry station, single blocks or the whole job have to be recreated on the monitor screen.

Gestaltungsterminals

Diese Geräte verfügen über einen Rechner und ein Satzprogramm. Sie arbeiten interaktiv; der Text kann nicht nur dargestellt, sondern gestaltet und im Darstellungsmodus direkt korrigiert werden.

Umbruchterminals

Ein Ganzseitenumbruch-System arbeitet interaktiv, das heisst, letzte Textkorrekturen können direkt am Umbruchbildschirm ausgeführt werden. Es gibt auch kombinierte Umbruch-/Gestaltungsterminals mit entsprechend unterschiedlicher Software.

Text- und Bildverarbeitungsterminals

Diese Ganzseitenterminals (Workstations) ermöglichen die integrierte Verarbeitung von Texten, Grafiken und Bildern zu kompletten Druckvorlagen (Gestaltung und Umbruch). Der hochauflösende Bildschirm zeigt permanent die echttypografische Gestalt der Arbeit neben der gewohnten Arbeitsbildschirm-Darstellung. Nebst Textbearbeitung können Grafiken und Reinzeichnungen direkt hergestellt werden, ebenso sind auch Bildbearbeitungsfunktionen möglich. Alles, was am Bildschirm ausführbar ist (zum Beispiel Rasterungen, Einrahmungen von Text- und Bildelementen, Unterlegen von Farbtönen usw.), muss auf dem Belichter auch tatsächlich ausgegeben werden können. Bildverarbeitung erfordert hohe Speicherkapazitäten und einen Laserbelichter.

Reproduktion

Flachbettscanner
Ein digitaler Schwarzweiss-Flachbettscanner tastet Strich- und Halbtonvorlagen ab und speichert die gescannten Vorlagen wahl-

Design Terminals

These units have both a computer and a typesetting program. They operate interactively, which means that the text can not only be displayed but also manipulated for design purposes and corrected directly in the display mode.

Make-Up Terminals

A whole-page make-up terminal operates interactively, which means that the final text corrections can be carried out directly on the make-up screen. There are also combined make-up and design terminals with correspondingly allocated software.

Text and Graphics Processing Terminals

These full-page terminals (workstations) make possible the integrated processing of texts, graphics and pictures to make complete originals for printing, by means of design and make-up. The high-resolution screen constantly shows the true typographic image of the job in addition to the usual screen display. In addition to the processing of texts, graphics and line drawings can be directy produced and picture processing functions are also possible. Everything that can be done on the screen (e.g. halftone screening, boxes and borders, tint laying, etc.) must be capable of actually being output on the exposure unit. Picture processing therefore requires a high computer storage capacity and a laser exposure system.

Reproduction

Flatbed Scanner
A digital, monochrome flatbed scanner scans line and tone originals and stores them either as line graphics, direct screening or

weise als Strichgrafik, als Direktrasterung oder Halbtoninformationen auf einer Festplatte. Die Bearbeitung erfolgt auf der Workstation.

Logoscanner
Der Logoscanner dient zum Digitalisieren, Korrigieren und Modifizieren von Zeichen und Schriften. Die gescannten Vorlagen können auf dem Bildschirm digital bearbeitet und auf einer Diskette gespeichert werden.

Speicherung

Magnetplattenspeicher
Auf Magnetplatten können umfangreiche Datenbestände abgelegt werden, die einen sofortigen wahlfreien Zugriff zu den gespeicherten Informationen erfordern. Je nach Modell kann ein Magnetplattenspeicher aus einer oder mehreren Platten bestehen. Mehrere Platten werden zu einem Plattenstapel zusammengefasst, welcher die Möglichkeit zum Auswechseln bietet. Festplatten können im Gegensatz zu den Wechselplatten nicht von einem Plattenwerk zum anderen ausgetauscht werden, sie sind im Plattenlaufwerk fest installiert.

Magnetbandstation
Unter diesem Begriff versteht man die gesamte Mechanik und Elektronik zur Steuerung und Bewegung des Magnetbandes sowie den Magnetkopf zum Schreiben und Lesen der Daten. Magnetbänder werden im Fotosatz ausschliesslich zu Datensicherungs- und Archivierungszwecken verwendet. Magnetbänder haben eine lange Zugriffszeit.

Drucker

Für Korrekturen können die verarbeiteten Daten als Klarschriftbelege (Hardcopy) auf einem Drucker ausgegeben werden. Damit können beispielsweise Belichtungen auf

contone information on a fixed disc. Operation is carried out at the workstation.

Logoscanners
The logoscanner serves for the digitization, correction and modification of signs and characters. The scanned copy can be treated digitally on the screen and stored on a floppy disc.

Storage

Magnetic Disc Store
Magnetic discs can be used for the storage of extensive quantities of data where immediate and free access to the stored information is required. A magnetic disc store may consist of one or several discs, in the latter case assembled into one group with the possibility of interchange. Unlike these interchangeable discs, fixed or hard discs cannot be interchanged between one unit and another but are permanently installed in the disc drive.

Magnetic Tape Stations
This term covers the entire mechanics and electronics of the control and movement of the magnetic tape and the magnetic head for reading and writing the data. In phototypesetting, magnetic tapes are used exclusively for purposes of data protection and archiving. Magnetic tapes require a lengthy access time, which means that whenever a given text from the middle of the tape is wanted, it must be wound to the appropriate position.

Print-Out

For correction purposes, the processed data can be output as hard copy on a printing device, providing savings, for example, in the use of photo materials. There are various

Fotomaterial eingespart werden. Es gibt verschiedene Typen von Druckern (zum Beispiel Thermodrucker, Matrixdrucker, Laserdrucker usw.), die nach unterschiedlichen technischen Prinzipien arbeiten. Über einen Plotter können ausser Text auch grafische Darstellungen ausgegeben werden.

kinds of printers (e.g. thermal, dot-matrix, laser), working in accordance with different technical principles. Where a plotter is used, graphics can be output as well as text.

Datenübernahme

Der Einsatz von Textsystemen, Minicomputern, Personalcomputern oder ganz allgemein von EDV-Systemen ermöglicht in zunehmendem Masse die Erfassung von Daten am Entstehungsort. Diese Daten brachte man früher als Manuskripte in die Setzerei. Heute können sie räumlich entfernt von ihrem Verarbeitungsort eingegeben und anschliessend (on line oder off line) an einem anderen Ort in ein anderes Gerät übertragen und weiterverwendet werden. Die Setzerei hat nun die Aufgabe, die angelieferten Daten zu interpretieren, typografisch aufzubereiten und in Satz umzuwandeln. Die Umwandlung erfolgt mittels Konverter. Hardwareseitig ist zusätzlich das Vorhandensein einer genormten Schnittstelle (Interface) erforderlich. Grundsätzlich werden heute für Datenübernahmen zwei Arten praktiziert: Übernahme per Datenfernübertragung (DFÜ) und ab Datenträgern (Disketten und Magnetbänder).

Data Transfer

The use of text systems, minicomputers, personal computers and electronic data processing systems in general is increasingly making it possible to input data at the place of origination, instead of sending copy to the typesetters in manuscript form as was formerly the rule. Nowadays, data can be input at a location remote from the place of processing, for subsequent on-line or off-line transfer to another location for further processing in another set of equipment. This gives the typesetting company the job of interpreting, marking-up and converting the data received into typographic output, using data conversion equipment. On the hardware side, a standard interface is also required. Today there are two basic ways of handling data transfer: remote data transmission and the delivery of data carriers (floppy discs and magnetic tapes).

Ausgabe

Unter Ausgabe sind lediglich die reinen Belichtungsanlagen zu verstehen.

Ziel des Fotosatzes ist es, nach der Texterfassung, Textverarbeitung und Korrektur eine fehlerfreie Belichtung auf fotografisches Material zu erhalten.

Die Belichtungseinheiten können off line oder on line angesteuert werden. Man unterscheidet zwischen optomechanischer Belichtung, CRT-Belichtung und Laserbelichtung.

Output

The term ''output'' covers only the final exposure or photo units.

The objective of photosetting is to obtain, after copy entry, processing and correction, an error-free exposure on photographic material.

Exposure units can be controlled on-line or off-line. A distinction is made between optical-mechanical, CRT and laser exposure units.

Optomechanische Belichtung

Ein optomechanischer Belichter besteht im wesentlichen aus folgenden Teilen: einem negativen Schriftbildträger (zum Beispiel Scheiben, Fonts oder Schriftrahmen), der von einer Lichtquelle (Xenon-Blitzlicht) durchleuchtet wird; einem optischen System, welches das Licht weiterleitet; sowie einer Vorrichtung, in der das zu belichtende Fotomaterial gehalten wird und nach der Belichtung entnommen werden kann. Der Breitentransport des Zeichens wird mechanisch unter Zuhilfenahme von optischen Einrichtungen vorgenommen. Die Information, wie breit das Zeichen transportiert werden soll (Dickte), liegt dem Rechner in Einheiten vor.

CRT-Belichtung

CRT ist die Abkürzung von *Cathode Ray Tube* (deutsch: Kathodenstrahlröhre).

Die Zeichen sind nicht gegenständlich, sondern elektronisch zerlegt, das heisst als Schwarzweissinformationen digital gespeichert.

Das Aufzeichnungsprinzip besteht im wesentlichen aus drei Teilen: die Kathodenstrahlröhre als Lichtquelle, ein optisches System und eine Fotomaterialbühne zum Festhalten und Transportieren des Fotomaterials. Von der Konstruktion her gesehen, findet man in CRT-Belichtern zwei Arten von Kathodenstrahlröhren. Die normale Kathodenstrahlröhre erfordert eine nachgeschaltete Optik; bei Kathodenstrahlröhren mit aufgesetzter Fiberglasoptik erfolgt die Belichtung direkt. Die Aufzeichnung erfolgt in vertikaler Richtung.

Optical-Mechanical Exposure

An optical-mechanical exposure unit consists principally of the following parts: a negative type image carrier (e.g. disc or frame) which is illuminated by a light source (xenon flash); an optical system which conveys the light; and a device to hold the material to be exposed and from which it can be removed after exposure. Lateral transport of the sign is carried out mechanically with the aid of optical devices. Information concerning the extent of lateral sign movement, i.e. set-width, is available to the computer in unit form.

CRT Exposure

CRT is the abbreviation for *Cathode Ray Tube*.

The typographic characters are held in electronic, not material form, as digital black-and-white information.

The principle of recording them involves three main parts: the CRT as light source, an optical system and an assembly to hold and transport the photo material. From an engineering point of view there are two types of CRTs in phototype exposure units, the normal kind which needs a subsequent optical system and the kind equipped with fibre-glass optics which expose directly. The characters are recorded vertically.

Laserbelichtung

Laser ist aus den Anfangsbuchstaben von *L*ight *A*mplification by *S*timulated *E*mission of *R*adation (deutsch abgekürzt: Lichtverstärkung).

Aufgrund des Aufzeichnungsprinzips sind auch die im Lasersatz verwendeten Zeichen digitalisiert. Gegenüber dem CRT-Satz erfolgt die Aufzeichnung nicht in vertikaler, sondern meistens in horizontaler Richtung. Mit Hilfe eines Lasers ist es möglich, das Licht auf einen sehr kleinen Punkt zu bündeln. Infolgedessen ist beim Belichtungsvorgang ein Punkt mit grosser Schärfe und Genauigkeit zu erzielen. Während beim CRT-Satz alle Zeichen nacheinander belichtet werden, geschieht die Belichtung beim Lasersatz zeilenweise, beziehungsweise seitenweise. Beim Lasersatz wird der Strahl grundsätzlich über das gesamte Format gelenkt. Die Steuerung des Laserstrahls kann auch umgekehrt werden, um wahlweise eine positive oder negative Belichtung zu erzielen.

Laser Exposure

The word laser is formed from the initials of *L*ight *A*mplification by *S*timulated *E*mission of *R*adiation.

On account of the principle of laser recording, this method also uses digitized characters. Unlike CRT setting, recording is usually carried out on a horizontal rather than a vertical plane. The laser makes it possible to focus light onto a very small point, with the consequence that a very sharp and precise dot can be obtained in the exposure process. Whereas by the CRT method all characters are exposed one after the other, laser exposure takes place line by line or page by page. Basically, the laser beam is deflected over the entire type area. Its control may also be reversed, so that either a positive or a negative exposure may be obtained.

Computerunterstützte (typografische) Gestaltung
von Robert Krügel-Durband

Computer-Aided (Typographic) Design
by Robert Krügel-Durband

«Der Homo televisionis mit seinen Sehgewohnheiten vom Fernsehen, Computerbildschirm und den Videoclips ist sich anderes gewöhnt als weiland der nur radiohörende, zeitungslesende Mensch der vorpostmodernen Ära.»

Ob einfaches Desktop-Publishing oder anspruchsvolle Gestaltung auf dem Computer, verheissen wird eine Technologie, welche die Kreativität rationalisiert, nach dem Motto: «Wer Computer bedienen kann, kann auch gestalten.» Das Versprechen ist trügerisch.

Von den begeisterten Anhängern der neuen Technologie wird gerne hervorgehoben, wie kreativ der Computer heute schon ist. Dies ist ein Missverständnis: Das zutreffende Attribut für den Computer ist nicht Kreativität, sondern dessen Fähigkeit, zur Kreativität anzuregen. Kreativ ist immer der Gestalter. Oder, um es mit dem Computerspezialisten Holger van den Boom zu sagen: «Nicht so sehr was der Computer kann, sondern wie er mich in meinem Können unterstützt, das macht zu guter Letzt seine Attraktivität aus.»

Was bringt der Computer dem Gestalter?

Während des Gestaltungsprozesses ist jedes Element sofort in einer dem Endresultat ähnlichen Qualität sichtbar.

In der Entwurfsphase sind stets gesamtgestalterische Zwischenresultate auf dem Bildschirm abrufbar, so kann jeder Schritt auf die Wirkung im Kontext überprüft werden.

Das Wechselspiel zwischen intuitivem Gestalten und rationalem Überprüfen und Entscheiden wird intensiver.

Der Gestaltungsprozess kann am Bildschirm direkter wahrgenommen werden, was eine komplexere und vielschichtigere Gestaltung ermöglicht.

''Homo Televisionis with his visual habits of television, display screen and video entertainment has different customs from the man of the former, prepostmodern era, accustomed only to newspaper reading and listening to the radio.''

Whether we consider basic desktop publishing or sophisticated graphic design on the computer screen, a technology which rationalizes creativity offers a promise, with the motto: ''Whoever can operate a computer can also design.'' This promise is false.

Devotees of the new technology are fond of pointing out how creative the computer is in itself. This is a misunderstanding. The relevant attribute of the computer is not creativity but the capacity to stimulate creativity. It is always the designer who is creative. In the words of the computer specialist Holger van der Boom: ''It is not so much what the computer can do as the way in which it supports my own abilities that really constitutes its great attraction.''

Of what benefit is the computer to the designer?

During the computer-aided design process, every element is immediately visible in a quality similar to that of the end product.

During the various stages of design, complete intermediate results can be called up to the screen at any time, so that every step can be checked for its effect within its context.

The interplay between intuitive design and rational monitoring and decision making becomes more intensive.

With the display screen the design process can be perceived more directly and intuitively, making more complex and more intricate designs possible.

Das Ausprobieren, die Suche nach unterschiedlichen Lösungswegen motivieren zum Gestalten in Bereichen, wo bisher der gestalterische Einsatz – weil zu aufwendig oder gar unmöglich – beschränkt war.

Text- und Bildebenen können komplex vernetzt und mit Strukturen versehen werden, Schriftzeichen ihrerseits als Bilder behandelt und durch nahezu unbeschränkte zwei- und dreidimensionale Modifikation zu neuen visuellen Erfahrungen führen.

Ein Entwurf ist immer gleichzeitig schon Endresultat, das heisst Rein- oder Druckvorlage.

Die Wege zur präzisen Visualisierung einer Idee verkürzen sich zum Teil, weil die grafischen und typografischen Elemente nicht mehr manuell erstellt werden müssen.

Für die Präsentation der Entwürfe können die erarbeiteten Materialien direkt verwendet werden, der Zeit- und Materialaufwand zur Herstellung einer Präsentation ist geringer.

Der Computer kann vieles. Aber er macht trotzdem nur das, was man ihm sagt. Dazu braucht es qualifizierte Gestalter, die mit ihm kompetent umzugehen wissen. Ein fundiertes Wissen um Schrift, Zeichen und Bild, die Beherrschung der Gestaltungsmöglichkeiten und ein kritisches Reflexionsvermögen sind neben den Bedienungstechniken unabdingbare Voraussetzungen für die gestalterische Arbeit am Computer. Leicht wird man sonst zum langweiligen Programmanwender.

Der Computerarbeitsplatz

Grundkonfiguration (Hardware)

Ein computerisierter Gestaltungsarbeitsplatz besteht heute im Minimum aus dem Computer selbst, der dazugehörenden Tastatur für die Eingabe von Text, einer Festplatte (Harddisk) als Speichermedium und einem

Trial and error and the search for different approaches provide the motive for designing in areas where formerly the scope of the designer was limited for reasons of time and cost, or even altogether impossible.

The levels of text and of graphics can be intricately interwoven and given new structures, while typographic characters can be treated as pictorial images, leading to new visual experiences through almost unlimited two- and three-dimensional modifications.

Every sketch is at the same time an end result, ready for printing or reproduction.

The pathway to the precise visualization of an idea is considerably shortened through the elimination of the manual production of graphic and typographic elements.

The material which has been worked on can be directly used for the presentation of a preliminary design, reducing the expenditure of time and material needed for presentations.

The computer can do many things, but only what it is told. Therefore qualified designers are needed who know how to use it competently. A well-grounded knowledge of type, signs and images, mastery of the possibilities of design and a capacity for critical reflection are essential prerequisites, together with the operating techniques, for creative design work on the computer. In default of these qualifications, one can quickly become a mere program user.

The Computer Workstation

Basic Configuration (Hardware)

Today, the minimum hardware for a computerized design workstation consists of the computer itself, its keyboard for the input of text, a hard disc as storage medium and an additional device for drawing by hand or con-

weiteren Bedienungsgerät, mit dem von Hand gezeichnet werden kann oder Befehle an den Computer weitergeleitet werden. Weiter gehören dazu ein hochauflösender Ganzseiten-Bildschirm und ein Laserdrucker.

veying commands to the computer. The equipment also includes a high-resolution, full-page screen and a laser printer.

Basiskonfiguration

Bildschirm
Computer

Basic

Display screen
Computer

Eingabegeräte

Zeichenbrett
Tastatur
Maus
Scanner

Input station

Drawing-board
Keyboard
Mouse
Scanner

Ausgabegeräte

Laser-Drucker
Belichtungsgerät
Diabelichter
Weitere

Output station

Laser-printer
Exposure unit
Transparency input
Further

Ergebnis

Papierausdruck
Papierbelichtung
Druckfilme
Dias

Result

Paper print-out
Paper exposure
Graphic films
Transparencies

Ausbau

Je nach Erfordernissen und Arbeitsschwerpunkten des Benutzers ist die Grundeinheit jederzeit mit neuen Geräten ausbaubar:

Auf der Eingabeseite (Input) kann ein elektronisches Zeichenbrett dazukommen oder ein Lesegerät (Scanner), das Zeichnungen,

Extensions

Depending on the user's requirements and pattern of work, the basic equipment can be extended at any time with the following items:

On the input side, an electronic drawing-board may be added, or a scanner to capture

Halbtonbilder, Dias oder Texte in grosser Feinheit zur Weiterbearbeitung auf dem Bildschirm erfasst.

Auf der Bearbeitungsebene sind zusätzliche Bildschirme für unterschiedliche Zwecke anschliessbar, monochrom oder farbig. Die Speicherkapazität für Daten kann mit weiteren Festplatten erweitert, das heisst der Arbeitsspeicher des Computers ausgebaut werden.

Die Ausgabeseite (Output) wird mit Laserdruckern mit höherer Auflösung, mit farbigem Ausdruck und/oder grösserem Druckformat aufgerüstet. Oder mit einer Belichtungsstation, die Fotosatzqualität in der Typografie, Magazinqualität in der Halbton-Bildwiedergabe ermöglicht.

Für andere Zwecke kann ein Belichtungsgerät angeschlossen werden, das Dias liefert, deren digitale Auflösungsfeinheit diejenige des Filmträgers übersteigt. Des weiteren sind Geräte erhältlich, die direkt Folien schneiden oder Prägestöcke gravieren.

Programme (Software)

Während es in der traditionellen Druckaufbereitung für die verschiedenen Arbeitsschritte jeweils einen Spezialisten benötigt (zum Beispiel Setzer, Reprofotograf, Retuscheur, Lithograf), erledigt der Gestalter mit dem Computer vieles selbst. Das Wissen und Können der Spezialisten wird nun durch ein Programm gewährleistet. Es hat gleichsam eine Vermittlerfunktion zwischen dem Gestalter, der etwas haben oder machen will, und dem Computer, der ihm das schnell und einfach ermöglichen soll.

Daher gibt es Programme für Texterfassung, Schriftentwurf, Grafik, Illustration, Retusche usw. Was mit diesen «Spezialisten»-Programmen entworfen und hergestellt wurde, verbindet ein Layoutprogramm zu einem Ganzen.

drawings, continuous tone pictures, transparencies and texts at fine resolution for further processing on the screen.

At the processing level, additional monochrome or colour screens may be connected for various purposes. The memory capacity for data can be extended with additional hard discs, i.e. the computer store can be enlarged.

The output side can be equipped with laser printers having finer resolution, printing in colour and/or on a larger sheet size. Alternatively, an imagesetter exposure station brings phototype quality to the text and magazine quality to the picture reproduction.

For other purposes, an exposure unit to produce colour transparencies may be connected, achieving a finer resolution than that of the film base. Other output devices may be used to cut foils or to engrave dies.

Programs (Software)

Whereas in traditional pre-press work a number of specialists are needed for different stages of the job (compositor, repro cameraman, retoucher, lithographic artist), the computer-aided designer performs a great many functions himself. The knowledge and ability of the specialist is replaced by a program, which also has an interactive function between the designer, who wants to have or do something, and the computer, which must respond to these demands quickly and easily.

Thus there are programs for copy entry, typeface design, graphics, illustration, retouching, and so on. Whatever is designed and produced by means of these "specialist" programs is assembled into a whole by means of a layout program.

Ungeachtet der Grösse einer typografischen Arbeit ist ein geordnetes Vorgehen unumgänglich. Wir müssen die uns gestellte Aufgabe, die Bedingungen und die Möglichkeiten genau kennen. Wir benötigen Informationen, die wir uns beschaffen oder die uns gegeben werden. Nur unter Berücksichtigung der ermittelten Fakten wird die gestalterische Arbeit sinnvoll und führt zu brauchbaren Resultaten.

Die folgende Gliederung ist ein Modell für einen möglichen Arbeitsablauf. Ein solches kann nicht vollständig sein, ist kein Rezept, da jede Aufgabe eine spezielle Vorbereitung verlangt und jeder Gestalter seine sehr persönlichen Methoden einfliessen lässt. Die drei Bereiche Vorbereitung, Gestaltung und Produktion sind jedoch als Basis für die Planung aller typografischen Arbeiten zu verstehen.

An orderly procedure is essential for any typographic job, however large or small. We must have an exact knowledge of the job in hand, the conditions and possibilities of its production. We need information, which we may obtain for ourselves or which may be given to us. The work of design can be meaningful and lead to usable results only when due account is taken of the information obtained.

The schedule proposed here is a model for the possible progress of a job. Such a model can never be complete, nor can it be taken as a recipe, since every job requires its own special preparation and every designer inputs his own very personal methods. Nevertheless, the three sectors of preparation, design and production should be taken as the basic framework for all typographic work.

1. Vorbereitung Dokumentation, Auswertung, Konzept	**1. Preparation** Documentation, evaluation, concept
1.1 Informationssender/Auftraggeber Tätigkeit, Produkte, Grösse, Bekannt- heitsgrad, Marktposition usw.	**1.1 Information Supplier/Client** Field of activity, products, size, extent of familiarity, market position, etc.
1.2 Informationsinhalt Art, Umfang, Tonalität, Struktur usw.	**1.2 Information Content** Nature, extent, colour scheme, structure, etc. of the content.
1.3 Informationsabsicht Verkauf, Orientierung, Überredung, Hilfe, Belehrung usw.	**1.3 Purpose of Information** Sales, orientation, persuasion, assis- tance, instruction, etc.
1.4 Informationsempfänger Junge, Alte, Männer, Frauen, spezielle Gruppen (beruflich, sozial, kulturell), Ausbildungsgrade, Kommunikations- gewohnheiten, Kaufkraftklassen usw.	**1.4 Information Receivers** Young people, old people, men, wom- en, special groups (professional, social, cultural). Educational level, communi- cations acceptance, income level, etc.
1.5 Informationsträger Printmedien (Zeitungen, Prospekte, Bücher, Plakate usw.), Lichtmedien (TV, Video, Filme usw.).	**1.5 Information Carriers** Print media (newspapers, brochures, books, posters, etc.), photo media (TV, video, films, etc.).
1.6 Satzproduktionstechnik Bleisatz, Fotosatz, Composersatz, Schreibmaschinensatz, Handschrift usw.	**1.6 Typesetting Technique** Metal typesetting, phototypesetting, Composer type, typewriter, handwrit- ing, etc.
1.7 Finanzen Ermitteln der Kosten und Budgeterstel- lung (Honorare und Produktion).	**1.7 Finance** Establishment of costs and preparation of a budget (fees and production).
1.8 Termine Die einzelnen Phasen sind zeitlich festzuhalten (Vorbereitung, Gestaltung, Produktion, Einsatz usw.).	**1.8. Deadlines** Progressive phases must be defined in terms of time (preparation, design, production, distribution, etc.).
1.9 Grobkonzept Zusammenfassen der Erkenntnisse und Darstellung der Projektidee (verbal und visuell).	**1.9 Broad Concept** Summary of facts known and presen- tation of the basic idea of the project (verbal and visual).

2. Gestaltung

2.1 Vorentwürfe
Skizzieren der verschiedensten typografischen Möglichkeiten. In dieser Phase sollten keine Einfälle unterdrückt oder verworfen werden, auch wenn diese im Moment unbrauchbar erscheinen.

2.2 Kritik der Vorentwürfe
Kritische Prüfung aller Vorentwürfe, Auswahl.
Nach der Kritik erfolgt nicht unbedingt die Phase der Produktion. Oft sind weitere ergänzende Skizzen notwendig. Oder man verlässt den eingeschlagenen Weg total und beginnt mit neuen Versuchen.

2.3 Entwurf für Präsentation
Bereinigung des ausgewählten Vorentwurfes.
Erstellen der Präsentationsvorlage (Maquette, Entwurf).

2.4 Präsentation

2. Design

2.1 Preliminary Designs
Roughs of the widest variety of typographical possibilities. At this stage no ideas should be suppressed or ruled out, even if they seem unusable at the time.

2.2 Appraisal of Preliminary Designs
Critical examination of all preliminary designs. Selection.
The production stage does not necessarily follow immediately after the appraisal. Further roughs in greater detail are often necessary: or the plan initiated may be completely discarded and new approaches taken.

2.3 Design for Presentation
Tidying up the selected preliminary design.
Production of the copy for presentation to the client (layout, dummy).

2.4 Presentation

3. Produktion

3.1 Vorbereitung der Produktionsphase

Terminkontrollen, Kostenkontrollen (Nachkalkulationen), Lieferantenbestimmungen usw.

3.2 Manuskriptbearbeitung

Manuskriptkontrollen (Lesbarkeit, grammatikalische Korrekturen usw.), Anweisungen für Satzproduktion, Texterfassung (EDV) usw.

3.3 Satzproduktion

(für Druck oder Bildschirm)
Satzherstellung, Satzkontrolle.
Produktion des weiterverwendbaren Materials:
a) Reproduktionsfähige Papierkopien für Reinzeichnungen.
b) Papierkopien für Umbruch.
c) Disquetten für Weiterbearbeitung auf dem Bildschirm.

3.4 Typomontagen

- Montage der Reinzeichnungen mit masshaltigen Papierkopien.
- Umbruch mit Papierkopien für Filmmontage.
- Detailgestaltung auf dem Bildschirm (CAD).
- Umbruch auf dem Bildschirm.

3.5 Vervielfältigungen

- Druckmedien.
- Lichtmedien.

3. Production

3.1 Preparation for Production

Checking deadlines, costs (re-calculation), supply requirements, etc.

3.2 Copy Preparation

Checking copy (legibility, grammatical corrections, etc.), typesetting instructions, copy entry (EDP terminal), etc.

3.3 Typesetting

(for print or screen)
Production, proofreading.
Production of materials for further processing:
a) Repro quality copies for artwork.
b) Photocopies (Xeroxes) for layouts.
c) Floppy discs for further processing on screen.

3.4 Type Assembly

- Assembly of artwork with dimensionally stable photostats.
- Make-up with photocopies for film assembly (layout).
- Design of typography details on screen or monitor (CAD).
- Page make-up on screen or monitor.

3.5 Mass Production

- Print media.
- Photo media.

Typografische Praxis
12 typografische Gestalter

Typography in Practice
12 Typographic Designers

Auch im Bereich der Typografie orientieren wir uns an Vorbildern. An «Vor-Bildern», Bildern, die «vor uns» entstanden sind. Die auch «vor uns» stehen können. Bilder, die uns aber auch überzeugen, die wir schätzen, die uns zu neuen Lösungen anregen.

Die auf den folgenden Seiten vorgestellten Gestalter mit Beispielen aus ihrem typografischen Werk sind eine sehr persönliche Auswahl. Zwölf Kapazitäten aus der viel grössern Gruppe einflussreicher typografischer Gestalter rund um die Welt. Die zwölf «Auserwählten» jedoch kenne ich alle, wir haben gemeinsam über Typografie in der Ausbildung wie in der Praxis diskutiert, Erfahrungen ausgetauscht und manchmal auch gestritten. Ihre Arbeiten zeigen einen lebendigen Ausschnitt aus der Vielfalt der typografischen Gestaltungsmöglichkeiten.

An dieser Stelle möchte ich für alle Beiträge, für die Beratung und Kritik bei der Zusammenstellung dieses Handbuches danken. Danken möchte ich auch meinem Lehrer Josef Müller-Brockmann. Er hat mir in der Ausbildung die gestalterischen Grundlagen vermittelt und mich über viele Jahre kritisch begleitet.

In typography, as in other fields, we obtain guidance from examples of good professional work. Examples that have come before us and stand before us as models which are not only convincing and valuable in themselves but also suggest new approaches to design.

The designers whose work is represented on the following pages have been selected by the author on a very personal basis. They show twelve different talents from the much wider spectrum of influential typographic designers around the world. However, I am personally acquainted with all the twelve selected artists and have discussed typography with them all in the contexts of training and of professional practice. We have exchanged experience and sometimes also upheld opposing views. Their works show a lively cross-section of the great diversity of possibilities in typographic design.

At this point I wish to express my thanks for all the contributions, advice and constructive criticism I have received in the compilation of the present book. I also wish to thank my teacher, Josef Müller-Brockmann, who taught me the groundwork of typography during my training and has taken a critical interest in my work over many years.

claus bremer
piktogramm, ideogramm, gedichtbild

claus bremer
pictograms, ideograms, pictorial poems

das piktogramm stellt dank vorgefundener form seinen vorgefundenen inhalt scheinbar oder tatsächlich in frage. beispiel: «taube». vorgefundene form: friedenstaube, heiliger geist. vorgefundener inhalt: mao («jeder gedanke, der ein nachlassen des kampfwillens verursacht oder eine geringschätzung des feindes bedeutet, ist falsch. kämpfen, unterliegen, nochmals kämpfen, wieder unterliegen, erneut kämpfen & so weiter bis zum sieg. das ist die logik des volkes.»). beispiel: «soldat». vorgefundene form: soldat aus dem dienstbüchlein, mit helm, gasmaske, aufgepflanztem bajonett. vorgefundener inhalt: («das gebot gebe ich euch, dass ihr einander liebt. dass, wie ich euch geliebt habe, auch ihr einander liebt! alle sollen's daran erkennen, dass ihr meine jünger seid, wenn ihr liebe zueinander habt. ja, das gebiete ich euch, dass ihr einander liebt. nicht sollst du töten, nicht sollst du stehlen, nicht sollst du als falscher zeuge aussagen. liebe deinen nächsten wie dich selbst!»).

ideogramme sagen formal, was sie inhaltlich sagen, & sagen inhaltlich, was sie formal sagen. ihre form ist ihr inhalt, ihr inhalt ihre form. beispiel: «immer schön in der reihe bleiben». das immer-schön-in-der-reihe-bleiben von immer-schön-in-der-reihe-bleiben ist anlass, nicht immer schön in der reihe zu bleiben, sondern sich von ihr zu lösen.

gedichtbilder lassen sich als bild betrachten oder als gedicht lesen. das *oder* macht das gedichtbild zum gedichtbild. Erst die bereitschaft der betrachtenden, das bild aufzugeben & die bildelemente als buchstaben oder buchstabengruppen zu lesen, wandelt das bild in eine fundgrube von gedichtfragmenten bzw. in ein gedicht, das – gelesen – wieder zum bild wird. gedichtbilder, frischhalte-packungen der poesie, schützen vor dem sog des konsums. beispiel: gedichtbild «mit der schere schreiben».

the pictogram, thanks to its given form, apparently or truly raises the question of its given content. example: "dove" pictogram. given form: dove of peace, holy ghost. given content: mao ("every thought that causes a weakening of the will to combat or signifies an underestimation of the enemy is false. to fight, to be defeated, to fight again, to be defeated again, to fight once more and so on until victory. that is the logic of the people.") example: "soldier" pictogram. given form: a soldier from the army booklet, with steel helmet, gas mask and fixed bayonet. given content: ("i command you to love one another, that you love one another as i have loved you! your love for one another will make it known to all that you are my children, for i command you to love one another. thou shalt not kill, thou shalt not steal, thou shalt not bear false witness. love thy neighbour as thyself!")

ideograms state through their form what is said by their content and their content is that which is expressed by their form. their form is their content and their content their form. example: ideogram for "always keep in good order". the good order of "always-keep-in-good-order" is a motive for not keeping in good order but escaping from it.

pictorial poems contain poems, in the sense of concealing and preserving them. they can be viewed as pictures or read as poems. it is this *alternative* that gives the pictorial poem its character. it is only the readiness of the viewer to ignore the picture and read its elements as letters or groups of letters that transforms the picture into a storehouse of poetic fragments or a poem which, once read, again becomes a picture. pictorial poems, preservative packaging of poetry, protect their content from the destructive power of consumption. example: pictorial poem "writing with scissors".

er Jed
danke Ge
'déř'déř
ein ein e
assen Nachl
s des des de   h se Nac
llens Kampfw   s   es des des
ht verursach   ursacht v   ht verursacht v
r oder oder o   de ode   oder oder oder ode
ne eine eine ei   n ein   ine eine eine eine ein
ätzung Gerings   zung Ge   ng Geringschätzung Ger
des des des des des   s des des   des des des des des des des
eindes Feindes Feindes Fein   indes Feindes Feindes F
bedeutet bedeutet be   tet bedeutet bedeutet be
ist'ist'ist'ist'ist'ist'ist'ist'ist' ist'ist'ist'ist'ist'ist'ist'is
sch falsch falsch falsch falsch falsch falsch falsch f
·····n·Kämpfen·Kämpfen·Kämpfen·Kämpfen·Kämpfen·Kämpfe
'terliegen'unterliegen'unterliegen'unterlieg''''
''s'nochmals'nochmals'nochmals'nochmals'no'''
kämpfen kämpfen kämpfen kämpfen kämpfen käm
e ieder'wieder'wieder'wieder'wi'der w
n unterliegen unterliegen unt
'neut'erneut'erneut'erneut'ein
kämpfen kämpfen kämpfen kämpf
und und und und und und und und
o so so so so so so so so so so
weiter weiter weiter weiter weit
is bis bis bis bis bis bis bis bis   te
zum zum zum zum zum zum zum
Sieg Sieg Sieg Sieg Sieg Sieg Sie ···
s'D's   Das Das Das
t ist ist i   ist ist ist i
d ei   e die die die
o i   ogik Logik L
es des d
ikes Vo
···

Das
t Gebot G
gebe gebe g
ch ich ich i
euch euch eu

aßs'dass'dass'da'
r ihr ihr ihr l
r ei einand ein
iebt li bt liebt lie leb
Dass'Dass'Dass'Dass'Dass'Dass'D'
e wie wie wie wie wie wie wie wie
ch ich ich ich ich ich ich ich ich
euch euch euch euch euch euch uch
iebt geliebt geliebt geliebt g eb
e habe habe habe habe habe habe be
h'auch'auch'auch'auch'auch'auch ch'
r ihr ihr ihr ihr ihr ihr ihr ih ihr
einander einander einander einan re
liebt li bt liebt liebt liebt bt
e'Alle'' e'Alle'Alle'Alle'Alle Al'
ollens   ens sollens sollens s
daran   n daran daran daran d
erken   rkennen erkennen erk
ss'das ass'dass'dass'dass'da
r ih   hr ihr ihr ihr ihr ihr
mein   meine meine meine meine m
ger J   ger Junger Junger Junger Jü
seid seid seid seid seid seid seid seid seid seid s
wenn'wenn'wenn'wenn'wenn'wenn'wenn'w''''' wenn'wenn'wenn'wenn w
ihr ihr ihr ihr ihr ihr ihr ihr   r ih   hr ihr ihr ihr ihr
e Liebe Liebe Li   Liebe Liebe Liebe Li   be
inander zueinan   ueinander zueinander z   be
t habt habt h   habt habt habt habt
a'Ja'Ja'J'   Ja'Ja'Ja'Ja'Ja'Ja'J
das das ge   das das das das das das
ete ge   ebiete gebiete gebiete
ich   h ich ich ich ich ich
eu   uch euch euch euch euch
''
dass'dass'dass'dass'dass'
ihr ihr ihr ihr ihr ihr ihr
er einander inander einande
liebt liebt   ebt liebt lieb
Nicht Nicht   t'Nicht'Nich
llst sollst   sollst sol
du du du du du   u du du d
ten töten töte   töten töte
ört'nicht'nic'   'icht'nicht
ollst soll   ollst soll
u du du du d   u du du du
ehlen stehle   len stehl
t'nicht'nic'   ht'nicht
ollst solls   st solls
du du du du d   u du du d
ls als als   alg als
lscher falsc   lscher fa
Zeuge Zeug   Zeuge Zeu
ssagen aus   agen aussagen a
e'Liebe Li   ebe'Liebe Liebe
en deinen   inen deinen
nsten nac   en nächst
e wie wie   wie w
ich dich   ich d
st sel   b
···

immer schön in der Reihe bleiben
immer schön in der Reihe bleiben
immer schön in der Reihe bleiben
immer schön in der Reihe bleiben
immer schön in der Reihe bleiben
immer schön in der Reihe bleiben
immer schön in der Reihe bleiben
immer schön in der Reihe bleiben
immer schön in der Reihe bleiben
immer schön in der Reihe bleiben
immer schön in der Reihe bleiben
immer schön in der Reihe bleiben
immer schön in der Reihe bleiben
immer schön in der Reihe bleiben
immer schön in der Reihe bleiben
immer schön in der Reihe bleiben
immer schön in der Reihe bleiben
immer schön in der Reihe bleiben
immer schön in der Reihe bleiben
immer schön in der Reihe bleiben
immer schön in der Reihe bleiben
immer schön in der Reihe bleiben
immer schön in der Reihe bleiben
immer schön in der Reihe bleiben
immer schön in der Reihe bleiben
immer schön in der Reihe bleiben
immer schön in der Reihe bleiben
immer schön in der Reihe bleiben
immer schön in der Reihe bleiben
immer schön in der Reihe bleiben
immer schön in der Reihe bleiben

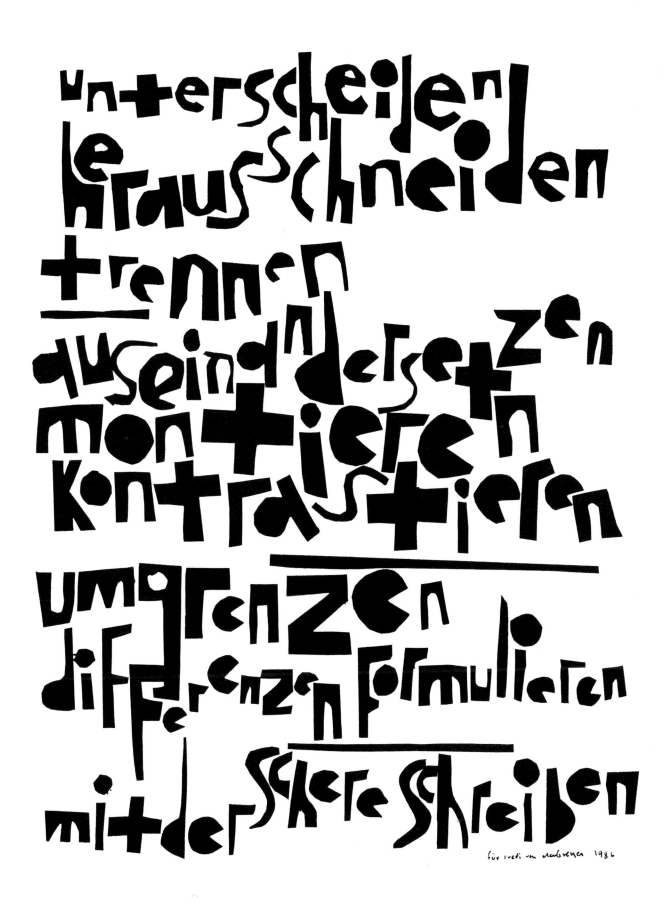

Giulio Cittato
Die provozierende Einfachheit

Giulio Cittato
A Provoking Simplicity

Im staubigen, halb verfallenen Triennale-Saal, wo sich enthusiastische Studenten zu lärmigen Gruppen zusammenfinden, fragt man sich, wie viele von ihnen sich in jüngster Zeit Gedanken über die Rolle des Designs gemacht haben. In nur wenigen Jahrzehnten ist das, was der grossen Masse visuelle Kommunikation und Produktedesign eröffnen sollte, zu einem der reichen Elite vorbehaltenen Luxusgut geworden.

Im Bereich des industriellen Designs ist diese Entwicklung weniger offensichtlich. Den verschiedenen Industrien ist es gelungen, zwischen dem Marketing eines Produktes und dem grundsätzlichen Spiel von Angebot und Nachfrage eine gezieltere Produkteauswahl vorzunehmen und auf weniger wirtschaftliche zu verzichten.

Bei der Kurzlebigkeit der heutigen visuellen Kommunikation machen einige wenige durch ihre deutliche Vorliebe für Klarheit und Einfachheit einen nachhaltigen Eindruck. Von diesen Exponenten hat namentlich Giulio Cittato (1936–1986) eine herausragende Rolle gespielt.

In the dusty, dilapidated hall of the Triennale where groups of noisy and enthusiastic students congregate, one wonders how many amongst them have asked themselves about the role of design recently. In just a few decades, what was supposed to bring visual communication and product design to the masses has become a luxury item reserved for the rich elite.

In the field of industrial design, the defeat is less obvious. Between the marketing of a product and the basic tenets of supply and demand, the industries concerned have managed to make a more precise selection of products while discarding the less economical ones.

In the effervescent world of today's visual communication, there are those who have made a deeper impression through their distinct preference for clarity and simplicity. Among these specialists, Giulio Cittato (1936–1986) played a prominent role.

7
Typografisches
Informationssystem
Typographical
information system

1

2

3

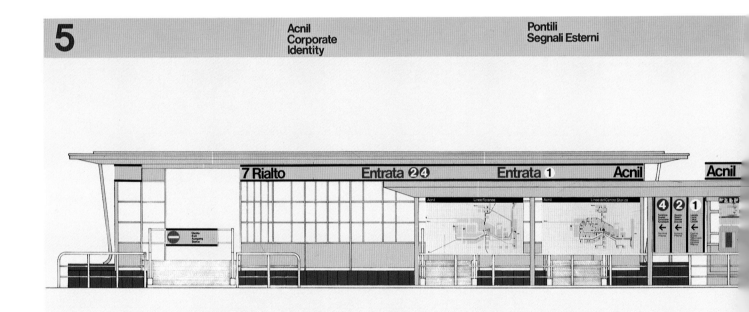

5   Acnil   Pontili
     Corporate   Segnali Esterni
     Identity

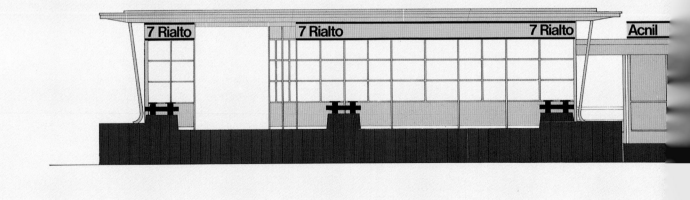

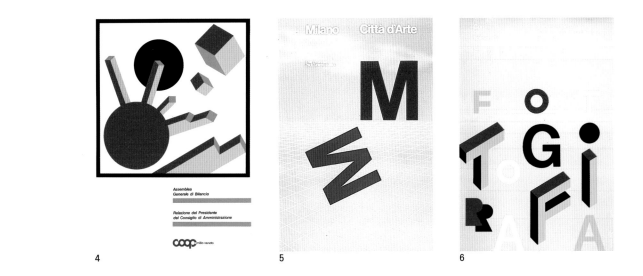

Assemblea
Generale di Bilancio

Relazione del Presidente
del Consiglio di Amministrazione

coop emilia-veneto

4

Milano   Città d'Arte

5

6

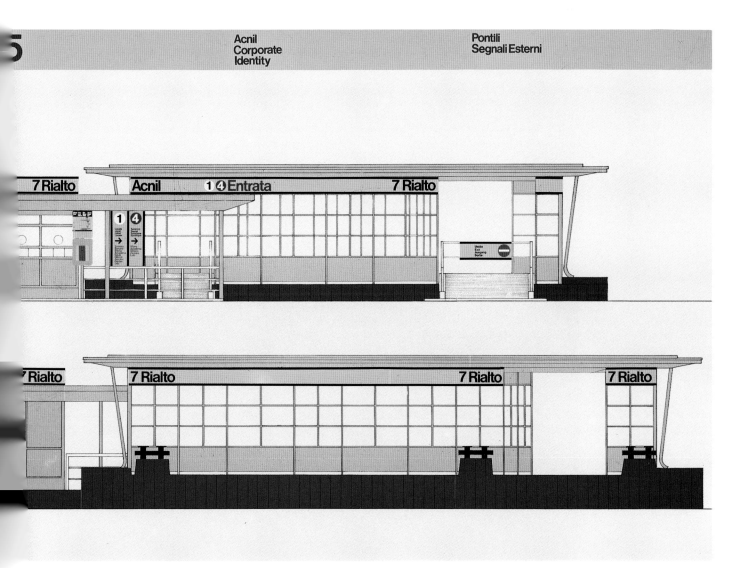

Acnil
Corporate
Identity

Pontili
Segnali Esterni

7 Rialto

Acnil   1 4 Entrata   7 Rialto

7 Rialto   7 Rialto   7 Rialto   7 Rialto

Mich interessieren der Raum und die Struktur in Verbindung mit Buchstaben oder Wörtern. Wenn ich ein Wort oder einen Buchstaben betrachte, will ich dessen Funktion als Überbringer der Bedeutung erhöhen. Indem ich Buchstaben und Wörter von ihren Beschränkungen befreie, kann ich sie deutlicher sehen.

Es kann eine vollkommen neue Welt geschaffen werden, indem ein zweidimensionaler Buchstabe, ein zweidimensionales Wort in einen dreidimensionalen Raum transponiert wird.

Ich experimentierte mit der «Design-Idee» mittels (Trans-)Formation von Buchstaben. Das Ziel des Designs besteht in anderen Worten darin, die unendliche Zahl von Gedanken in möglichst vielen Variationen darzustellen. Alle Variationen werden auf einem soliden dreidimensionalen Rastersystem dargestellt, wodurch sie durch eine mathematische Ordnung miteinander verknüpft sind.

I am interested in space and structure contingent to letters or words. Looking at a word or a letter, I want to transcend its function as the transmitter of meaning. By freeing letters and words from their restrictions, I am able to see them more clearly.

A totally new world can be created by transposing a two-dimensional letter or word into a three-dimensional space.

I experimented on the "idea of design" through the (trans) formation of letters. In other words, the aim of design is to present the infinite ideas in as many variations as possible. All variations are designed on a three-dimensional solid grid system, and thus are interrelated through mathematical order.

1
Aluminiumskulptur
Aluminium sculpture

2
«A» aus dem
Spiegelalphabet
"A" from the
Mirror alphabet

1

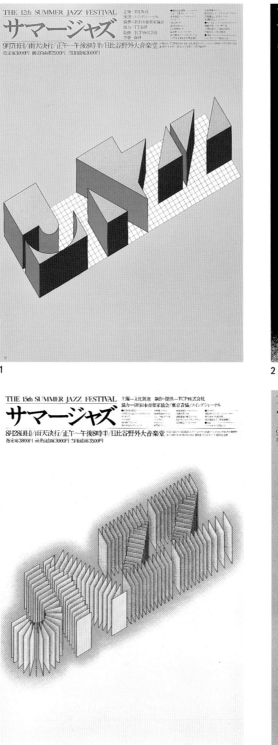

1

2

3

4

1–4
Plakatserie
Poster series

Wortmarke als System
Logotype as system

In unserem Studio nimmt der Computer einen grossen Stellenwert ein. Anfängliche Skepsis gegenüber dem «nützlichen Idioten» in der Gestaltung verwandelte sich immer mehr in die Einsicht, dass er nicht einfach nur ein zusätzliches Handwerkszeug ist, sondern ein Denkwerkzeug, mit dessen Hilfe der gestalterische Alltag neu erfunden werden kann.

Dass ich ein bis anhin materialgebundenes Ausdrucksmittel jetzt in immaterieller Form am Bildschirm einsetze und manipuliere, lässt mich den Reiz des Neuen spüren – und mich von Konventionen lösen: Inhalte müssen sich nicht zwangsläufig über den Wortlaut mitteilen, Typografie wird zur Bildsprache. Vielleicht auf Kosten der «Lesbarkeit», aber zugunsten meiner gestalterischen Individualität und einer stärkeren Memorierbarkeit.

Gleichzeitig passiert etwas Interessantes: Der Umstand, dass ich als Gestalter am Computer alle Details einer Arbeit (bis hin zu Durchschuss, Laufweite und Schriftgrösse) nach dem Trial-and-Error-Prinzip unmittelbar klären kann, schlägt sich in einem sich laufend vertiefenden Verständnis über Bedeutung und Eigenleben von Zeichen und Wort nieder. Die typografische Sensibilität, das Gestaltungsrepertoire und die Sicherheit und der Mut im Umgang damit wachsen ständig. Vielleicht liegt hier der Schlüssel dazu, wie künftig das Erlebnis Typografie in unserer komplexen Bilder-Gesellschaft hautnah und lustvoll vermittelt und erfahren werden kann.

In our studio, the computer has an important part to play. Initial scepticism about the ''useful idiot'' has been transformed into an understanding that the computer is not just an additional manual instrument but an instrument of the mind, with whose aid the daily work of design can be discovered anew.

The ability to use and manipulate a means of expression, hitherto material in its nature, in an immaterial form on the screen, now gives me the thrill of novelty. The new way of working also releases me from old conventions concerning the necessity of conveying the content strictly by means of the wording: typography is now becoming a visual language, perhaps at some cost to ''legibility'' but to the advantage of my creative individuality and a greater memorability in the resulting design.

At the same time there has been an interesting development. The fact that the designer working at the computer can immediately clarify all the details of a job, right down to the amounts of line spacing, length of lines and type size, by the trial-and-error principle, is reflected in a continuously deepening understanding of the significance and independent life of signs and words. All this gives a constant growth to one's typographical sensibility, creative repertoire and confidence and boldness in making use of it. Perhaps this aspect of computer-aided design provides the key to the ways in which it will become possible to convey and receive the typographical experience intimately and pleasurably in the complex, image-literate society of the future.

Sur son pourtour, le soleil
rayonne à 6000 degrés.
Mais lorsque ses rayons attei-
gnent la terre, au terme d'un
long voyage dans l'espace,
ils ne fournissent plus qu'une
prestation de 1 kilowatt par
mètre carré. Lorsque le ciel
est gris, elle tombe même à
20 watts.

Nous   nous   branchons   sur le soleil

C'est là le grand inconvénient
de l'utilisation de l'énergie solaire sous nos latitudes: l'in-
solation est irrégulière.
En outre, elle est brève l'hiver
durant et nulle pendant la nuit.
De l'énergie solaire qui par-
vient jusqu'à notre planète,
nous pouvons tirer parti et
profit de deux composantes:
la chaleur et la lumière.

Chauffage par four solaire

On peut faire un usage passif
ou actif de la chaleur solaire.
L'utilisation passive de la chaleur solaire signifie que des me-
sures d'architecture et des
techniques de construction
(isolations, jardins d'hiver, élé-
ments d'accumulation, etc.)
empêchent le bâtiment de ray-
onner immédiatement la chaleur qu'il a emmagasinée sous
l'effet du soleil.
On peut économiser de la sorte
jusqu'à la moitié des frais de
chauffage.

Dans la technique solaire active,
dite thermique, la chaleur solaire est accumulée, par exemple dans des collecteurs plats
ou en forme de tubes, qui
sont remplis d'eau ou d'huile.
La chaleur solaire ainsi con-
centrée alimente des chauffa-
ges et sert également à chauf-
fer l'eau.Certains collecteurs
spéciaux à conduits miroités
ou munis de réflecteurs per-
mettent d'obtenir des tempé-
ratures très élevées à partir
desquelles il y a production
de vapeur et de courant électrique.

Du courant tiré de la
lumière solaire
voir les examples des pages 7 et 8

Le silicium, élément naturel,est,
après l'oxygène, celui qui est
le plus répandu sur terre. Il
est semblable aux métaux et
on le trouve avant tout com-
me élément de liaison dans le
sable et le quartz. La particu-
larité du silicium pur est sa
sensibilité à la lumière. La lumière pénétrant dans l'atome
de silicium produit de l'électricité qu'il est possible de dé-
river. On appelle ce phénomè-
ne l'effet photovoltaïque (c'est-
à-dire la transformation de la
lumière en électricité).
Premières applications: les
posemètres des appareils pho-
tographiques. Plus tard, de
telles cellules photosensibles
ont servi à approvisionner les
satellites en courant electri-
que. Et, finalement, on a com-
mencé à fabriquer des cellules solaires pour la production de courant électrique en
plus grande quantité.

L'inconvénient majeur des cellules solaires est leur prix. Ce-
lui-ci s'explique par les techniques de fabrication com-
plexes que nécessitent les cellules à base de silicium ultra-
pur. Le coût par kilowattheure
de l'énergie produite de cette
façon n'est actuellement pas
concurrentiel avec le coût du
kilowattheure produit par des
centrales hydro-électriques ou
nucléaires.
Les laboratoires de recherche
persèvèrent donc actuellement dans leurs efforts pour
mettre au point des techniques de fabrication meilleur
marché.

Autre handicap: l'absence de
possibilités de stockage - à la
fois économiques et pratiques-
de l'électricité obtenue à partir des cellules solaires, appe-
lées aussi capteurs. On espère
parvenir à développer de nou-
veaux accumulateurs, plus petits, plus légers et plus per-
formants que les batteries tra-
ditionnelles, toujours lourdes
et encombrantes.

En Suisse, il n'est guère question de construire de vérita-
bles centrales pour produire
en masse de l'électricité d'ori-
gine solaire.
En revanche, des solutions
décentralisées à base de capteurs solaires à installer en
toiture des bâtiments ou à
d'autres endroits disponibles
ont certainement de l'avenir.

A l'heure actuelle, la production
de courant électrique d'ori-
gine solaire est d'ores et déjà
rentable pour de petits con-
sommateurs dont le raccorde-
ment au réseau d'alimentation
en électricité serait très
coûteux.
voir les examples en pages 7 et 8

é   n   e r g i e
s   l   a   i r e

**Les entreprises électriques
sont dynamiques**

Des compagnies et centrales d'électricité en
nombre croissant fabriquent des installations à base de cellules solaires ou partici-
pent à des études et projets émanant de
communes, d'entreprises et de particuliers.
Il s'agit, entre autres, de:

Société Romande d'Electricité (SRE)
voir exemple page 8
Entreprises Electriques Fribourgeoises (EEF)
Centraleschweizerische Kraftwerke (CKW)
Elektrizitätswerk Murg (SG)
voir exemple page 7

Zeitschrift
Magazine

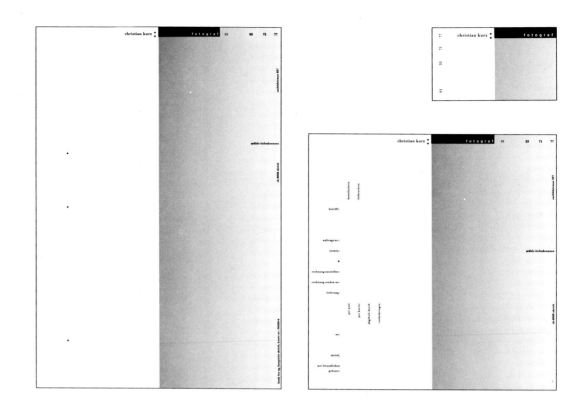

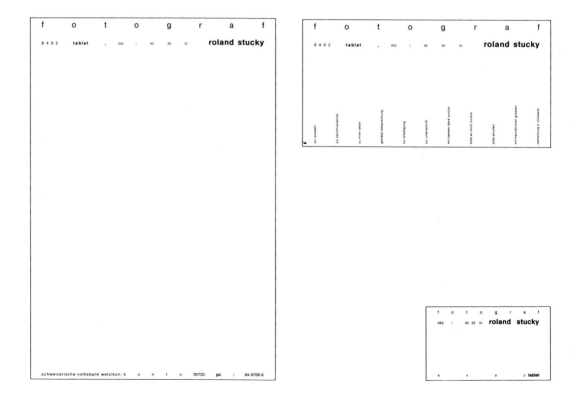

Geschäftsdrucksachen
Business stationery

Entwicklungsstufen
einer Wortmarke
Design phases of
a logotype

Frans Lieshout (Total Design)
Die Typografie als visuelle Erfahrung

Frans Lieshout (Total Design)
Typography as Visual Experience

Frans Lieshout zeigt in seinem Werk eine starke Vorliebe für eine Typografie, die nicht von den herkömmlichen Prinzipien der Anordnung von Text und Bild eingeschränkt wird.

Einzelne Buchstaben und Satzzeichen, Wörter, Sätze und Satzblöcke stellt er als illustrative Komponenten zu einer lebendigen und phantasievollen Komposition zusammen.

Damit will er nicht kommentieren: Er will beim Betrachter Eindrücke hervorrufen, Eindrücke verstärken. Mit seinen breitangelegten visuellen Experimenten will er über die reine Information hinausgehen und dadurch die Aufmerksamkeit der Leserschaft wecken und in seinen Bann ziehen.

Das Ergebnis ist stets ein sehr originelles Bild, das dem heute gängigen Funktionalismus eine unerwartete, packende Bedeutung verleiht.

Zu seinem persönlichen Typografiestil meint Lieshout: «Meine Layouts sind ganz eindeutig illustrativ. Die Typografie ist für mich nicht einfach ein Mittel, um den Text so aufzumachen, dass seine Botschaft möglichst deutlich ausfällt. Die Typografie ist für mich ebenso ein Mittel, um diese Botschaft zu verstärken, sie visuell attraktiv zu gestalten. Auf diese Art wird das Druckerzeugnis zugänglicher für den Leser, aber gleichzeitig auch offener für Experimente.»

In his work Frans Lieshout shows a strong interest in the typographical approach not limited by traditional ordering principles for text and images.

Individual letters and punctuation marks, words, sentences and blocks of type he treats as illustrative components in a vivid and imaginative composition. Not with the purpose to comment but rather to confirm or enhance.

Within the broad scope of his visual experiment he aims to create a surplus to the information, triggering the attention of the public and holding it.

The result is always a very original image that gives an interesting and intriguing new meaning to present-day functionalism.

Lieshout expresses himself as follows on the subject of his typography: ''My layouts have a distinctly illustrative character. For me, typography is not only a means of arranging text so as to make its messages as clear as possible, but also a means of strengthening the message or making the text visually attractive. In this way the printed matter becomes more accessible to the reader and at the same time more open to experimentation.''

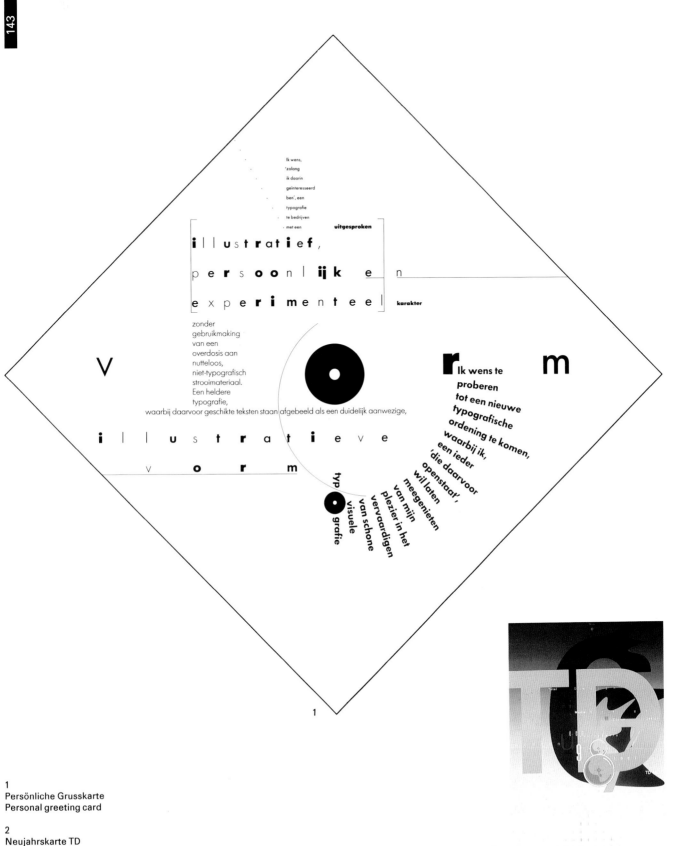

Ik wens,
'zolang
ik daarin
geinteresseerd
ben', een
typografie
te bedrijven
met een   **uitgesproken**

il**l**us**t**ra**t**i**e**f,

pe**r**s**oo**n**l**ij**k**   e   n

e**x**p**e**r**i**m**e**n**t**ee**l**   **karakter**

zonder
gebruikmaking
van een
overdosis aan
nutteloos,
niet-typografisch
strooimateriaal.
Een heldere
typografie,
waarbij daarvoor geschikte teksten staan afgebeeld als een duidelijk aanwezige,

V

o

r   m

rIk wens te
proberen
tot een nieuwe
typografische
ordening te komen,
waarbij ik,
een ieder
'die daarvoor
openstaat',
wil laten
meegenieten
van mijn
plezier in het
vervaardigen
van schone
visuele
typ**o**grafie

il**l**us**t**ra**t**i**e**v**e**

v   **o**   **r**   m

1

1
Persönliche Grusskarte
Personal greeting card

2
Neujahrskarte TD
New-Year's card TD

2

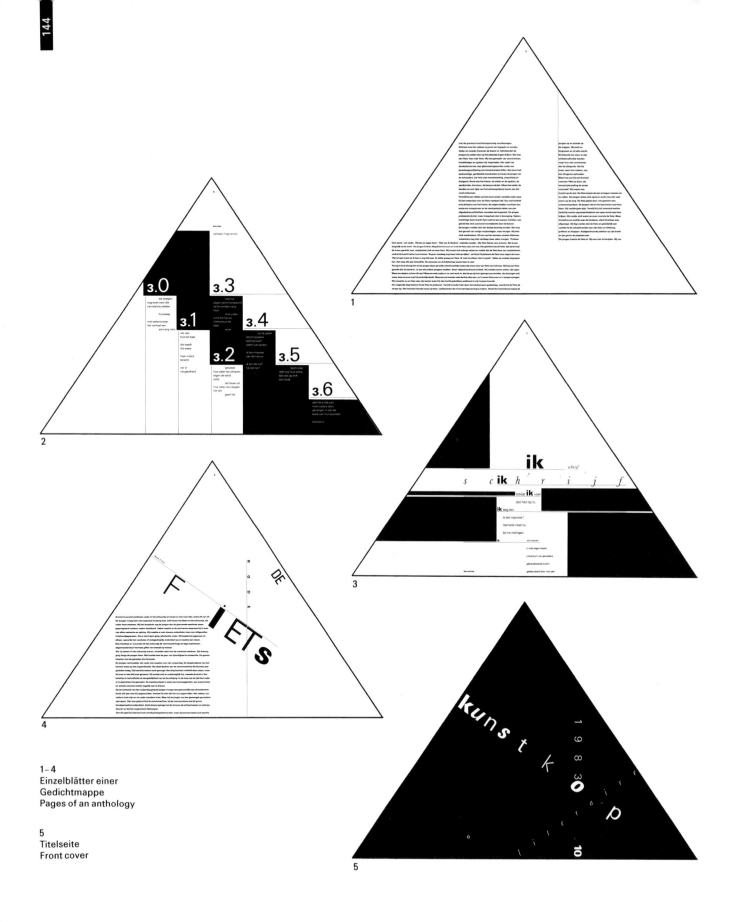

1–4
Einzelblätter einer
Gedichtmappe
Pages of an anthology

5
Titelseite
Front cover

typografie is de ordening van tekst op papier

Typografie van drukwerk

Typografie is de ordening van tekst op papier. Deze ordening kan er bij eenzelfde tekst heel verschillend uitzien omdat de mogelijkheden binnen de typografie van drukwerk zo gevarieerd zijn. De diversiteit bij verschillende soorten teksten is nog groter. De ordening van tekst op een formulier is nu eenmaal een andere dan die in een jaarverslag, zoals de ordening van tekst in een literatuurlijst er weer anders zal uitzien dan die van een promotiefolder. Voor de huisstijl van het Ministerie van Onderwijs en Wetenschappen zijn een aantal typografische richtlijnen ontwikkeld die in hun toepassing ervoor zorgen dat een bepaalde typografische kwaliteit gewaarborgd is en die ervoor zorgen dat het drukwerk van het ministerie herkenbaar is. Heel kenmerkend zijn de horizontaal verspringende tekstblokken, zoals toegepast in deze brochure. De typografische richtlijnen kunnen een zeer dynamische, contrastrijke of gevarieerde typografie mogelijk maken, maar evengoed een ingetogen of bescheiden typografie. De richtlijnen zijn duidelijk en gedetailleerd, in veel gevallen zelfs erg strikt. Ze kunnen zelfs zó strikt zijn dat nauwkeurig omschreven wordt hoe aanhalingstekens gezet moeten en hoe opsommingen in de tekst genummerd dienen te zijn. Maar waar het gaat om de ordening van de tekst wordt weer veel ruimte gelaten aan de individuele ontwerper. Het is dan ook niet zo dat in de typografie geen plaats voor creativiteit zou zijn.

Het is dan ook niet zo dat in de typografie geen plaats voor creativiteit zou zijn

Sprache ist unser wichtigstes Kommunikationsmittel . . . und Typografie macht sie lesbar. Typografische Gestaltung produzieren und konsumieren wir also jeden Tag. Trotzdem haben sich dafür immer nur wenige interessiert. Das ändert sich heute. Es rückt ins Bewusstsein,

– dass eine verbale Botschaft durch ihre typografische Gestaltung interpretiert, in ihrem Sinn vielleicht völlig verändert wird.

– dass der Gebrauch der beiden Informationsebenen Text und Bild besser aufeinander abgestimmt werden sollte – und die starre Grenze dazwischen durchlässiger gestaltet werden könnte.

– dass Forschung im Bereich visueller Kommunikation nicht nur der Werbung (die mit den dadurch erworbenen Erkenntnissen vor allem etwas verkaufen will) und den in linguistischen Seminaren ghettoisierten Semiotikern überlassen werden soll.

– dass typografische Gestaltung so gesehen eine enorm politische Dimension hat, die weitgehend unerkannt ist.

Language is our most important means of communication . . . and typography makes it readable. Thus we produce and consume typographical design every day. Nevertheless, only a few people have taken an interest in the subject at any time. The situation is changing today as people become conscious of the fact that:

– A verbal message is interpreted by means of its typographical design and perhaps has its meaning completely changed.

– The use of the two levels of information, textual and pictorial, should be better integrated and the usual fixed boundary between the two could be made more penetrable.

– Research in the field of visual communication should not be left only to the advertising world (which by means of the knowledge thereby gained above all wants to sell something) and the science of semiotics in its ghetto of linguistic seminars.

– Typographical design seen in this way has a vast political dimension which is largely unrecognized.

Abbildungen:
Aus dem Buch «Typo»,
Ausbildung in typografischer Gestaltung,
von Hans-Rudolf Lutz, Zürich

Illustrations:
From the book ''Typo''
Education in typographic design,
by Hans-Rudolf Lutz, Zurich

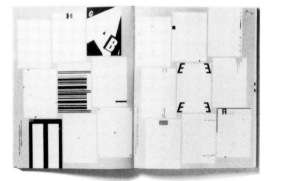

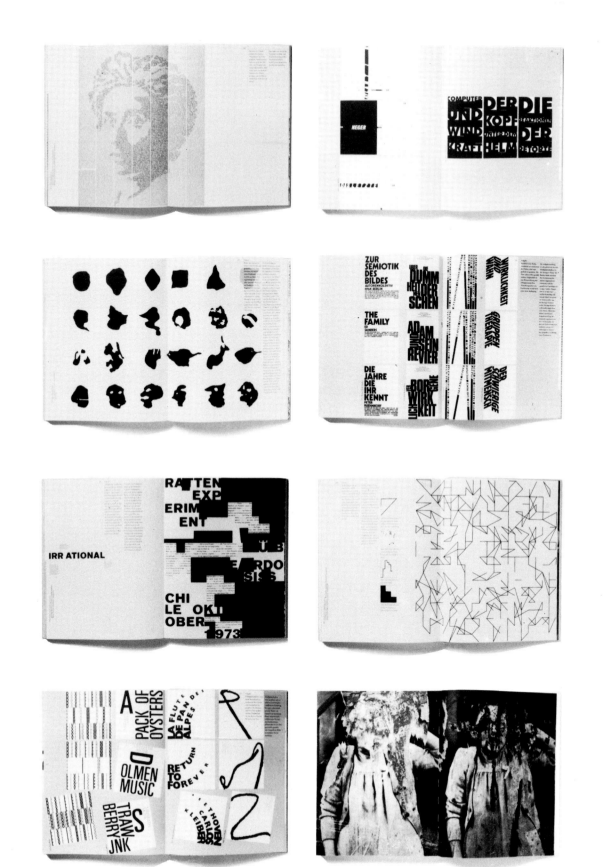

Pierre Mendell

Pierre Mendell

«Die Typografie dient der rationalen Mitteilung einer Botschaft.»
«Die Gestaltung der Typografie schafft das emotionale Umfeld für diese Botschaft.»

«Für Pierre Mendell scheint die Fähigkeit nichts Ungewöhnliches zu sein, das entscheidende und visuell interessante Element eines Themas oder Produktes klar hervorzuheben. Das ist aber nur der Anschein. Profundes Suchen, Zeit, Intelligenz und Talent sind die Voraussetzungen für diese Einfachheit.
Die Ergebnisse seiner Arbeit sind deswegen so bemerkenswert, weil jede mit einer Idee beginnt, die sowohl aus dem Thema als auch aus einer grafischen Vorstellung entspringt. In den Themen, für die er eine Anzeige, einen Einband oder ein Plakat entwickelt, erkennt er die Grundformen der Gestaltung. Dann nutzt er diese Formen meisterhaft. Pierre Mendell beginnt mit dem, was visuell offensichtlich ist. Steht jedoch kein Bild zur Verfügung, wendet er sich instinktiv der Schrift und starken, reinen Farben zu und setzt diese in seine grafische Kunst um, die beispielhaft ist.»

Ivan Chermayeff, New York

''Typography serves for the rational communication of a message.''
''Typographic design provides the emotional environment for this message.''

''For Pierre Mendell, the ability to bring out clearly the decisive and visually interesting element of a subject or product seems nothing out of the ordinary, but that is only a semblance. Deep searching, time, intelligence and talent are the necessary conditions for this simplicity.

The results of his work are so remarkable because each job begins with an idea deriving both from the subject matter and from a graphic concept. In the subjects for which he develops an advertisement, a book cover or a poster, he recognizes the basic elements of the design, then uses these elements in a masterly way. Pierre Mendell begins with what is visually obvious. Where no pictorial image is available, he instinctively turns to lettering and strong, pure colours, converting these into graphic art of an exemplary character.''

Ivan Chermayeff, New York

Warenzeichen
für Kinder-Sportschuhe
Logotype for
children's sports shoes

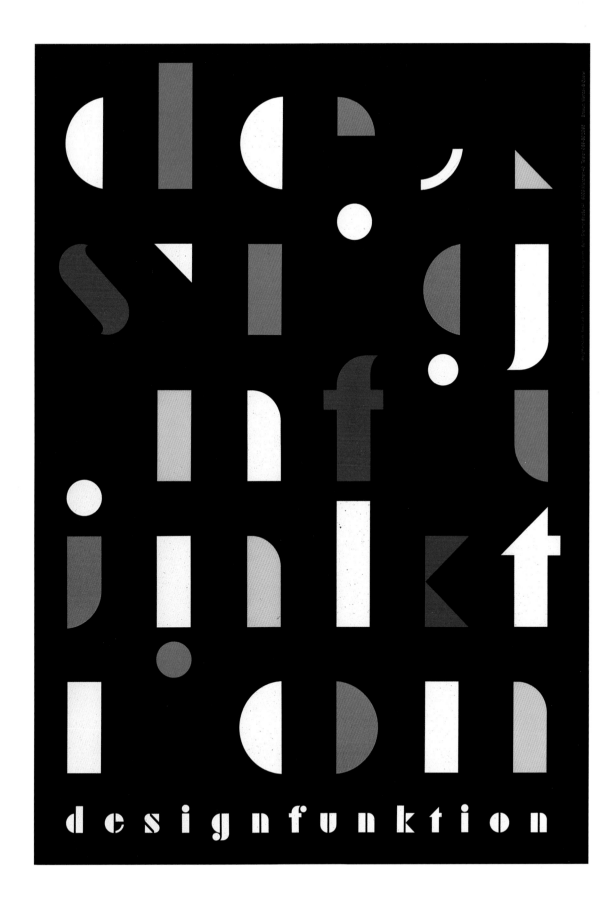

● Richard Hey ●
Ohne Geld singt
der Blinde nicht
●●● Roman ●●●
AutorenEdition

1

Walter Jens

Der Untergang

Kindler

2

Parkemed

Schmerz und Entzündung – Entzündung und Schmerz: Rp. Parkemed
Lange Jahre intensiver Forschungsarbeit waren nötig, bis Parkemed, eine Einzelsubstanz aus einer für
Analgetika völlig neuen Substanzklasse entwickelt werden konnte. Der zweifache therapeutische Effekt
wird durch die ausgeprägte analgetische und gleichzeitig entzündungshemmende Wirkung erreicht. Besonders
bewährt hat sich Parkemed bei Weichteilschmerzen und Muskelschmerzen, Schmerzen bei Arthrose und anderen
Erkrankungen des rheumatischen Formenkreises. Parkemed ist in der empfohlenen Dosierung ausgezeichnet
verträglich – auch von Seiten des Magendarmtraktes – entscheidend gerade für eine langfristige Therapie.
Packungen mit 12 und 30 Kapseln zu 250mg Mefenaminsäure. Flasche mit 60ml Suspension. PARKE-DAVIS

3

soskinderdorf

4

1, 2
Buchumschläge
Book jackets

3
Inserat
Advertisement

4
Plakat
Poster

Bruno Monguzzi

In seinen «Typographischen Tatsachen», die 1925 zu Ehren Gutenbergs in Mainz erschienen, hält El Lissitzky fest, dass «die typographische Plastik durch ihre Optik das tun soll, was die Stimme und die Geste des Redners für seine Gedanken schafft».

Diese innere Verwandtschaft der Arbeit des Typografen mit jener des Redners – oder genauer noch: mit jener des Schauspielers – bleibt die gültigste und intelligenteste Herausforderung für den angehenden Grafikdesigner, der sich, jenseits der Grenzen des Kommunizierens, leicht in den Windungen der Moden verirrt.

El Lissitzky, in his ''Typographical Facts'' (''Typographische Tatsachen'') published in Mainz in 1925 in honour of Gutenberg, asserted that ''typographical design should perform optically what the speaker creates through voice and gesture for his thoughts''.

This assimilation of the work of the typographer with that of the orator, or better, with that of the actor, remains the most relevant and intelligent provocation among the confrontations of young students, always side-tracked in the maze of fashion beyond the confines of communication.

Plakat
Poster

? . B B B B B B B B B B

di baci

di volte al diavolo,
sono (false) esagerazioni,
cioè «iperboli».

Il linguaggio moderno,
ricco di esagerazioni,
è senza alcun dubbio
un linguaggio iperbolico.

1.000.000.000.000.000.000

Dire: «ti mando

oppure ti mando»

Si esagera con grandiosità, nel buono e nel cattivo.

iperbole

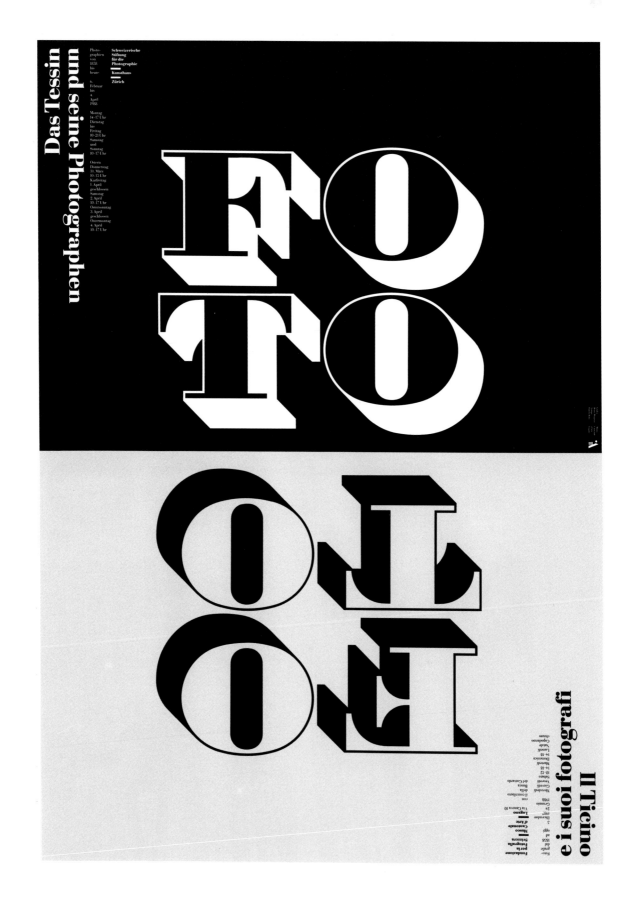

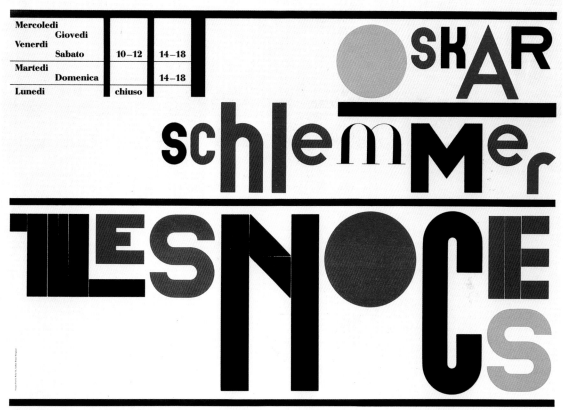

Mercoledi	Giovedi			
Venerdi	Sabato	10–12	14–18	
Martedi	Domenica		14–18	
Lunedi		chiuso		

OSKAR schlemMer

LES NOCES

Scenografie, acquerelli, disegni, documenti per la musica di

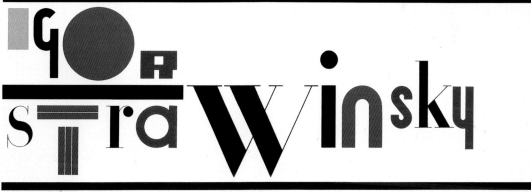

IGOR STRAWINSKY

Museo Cantonale d'Arte, Via Canova 10, Lugano   2 Luglio–2 Ottobre 1988

Ein Mann und eine Frau. Siegfried Odermatt und Rosmarie Tissi. Seit 1968 haben sie ein Gemeinschaftsatelier. Sie arbeiten auf kleinstem Raum, ohne Personal und Maschinerie. Jeder hat seine eigenen Aufträge, jeder berät und fordert den andern auf seine Art heraus. Gemeinsam ist beiden eine über Jahre konstante handwerkliche Präzision ebenso wie die kontinuierliche Weiterentwicklung ihres immer wiedererkennbaren Gestaltungskonzeptes: klare und schöne Aussagen zu machen, ohne das Auge zu langweilen oder aber vom Lesen abzubringen. Gemeinsam ist beiden auch ein stolzes Selbstbewusstsein, mit ihren Mitteln und ihrer Disziplin nicht jede x-beliebige Gestaltungsaufgabe lösen zu können und zu wollen, sondern mit ein paar «guten Arbeiten» pro Jahr erfolgreich zu sein, für den Auftraggeber, die Öffentlichkeit und . . . sich selber. Bei aller Gemeinsamkeit haben Siegfried Odermatt und Rosmarie Tissi aber ihre eigenen gestalterischen Spezialitäten, eine Vorliebe oder ein Faible: Während er sehr oft mit Linien und Balken, Winkeln und den dabei entstehenden Hell-Dunkel-Kontrasten arbeitet, verwandelt sie ebenso oft die Fläche in optischen Raum, schafft Raumillusionen.

Rolf Müller, München

A man and a woman. Siegfried Odermatt and Rosmarie Tissi. They have shared a studio since 1968. They work in minimal space, without staff or machinery. Each one has his or her own commissions and advises and stimulates the other with thought-provoking comments. What they have in common is a manual precision, kept constant over many years, and a continuous development of their ever-recognizable concept of design: making clear and elegant statements, without tiring the observer's eye or distracting it from the reading matter. They also share a proud self-confidence in not wishing to devote their capacities and discipline to any commission that may be offered but to being successful with just a few "blue-chip" jobs per year: successful for the client, for the public and . . . themselves. With all their common interests, Siegfried Odermatt and Rosmarie Tissi each have their own "designer" speciality, a preference or a weakness. Whereas he very often works with thin and thick rules, angles and the resulting light-and-dark contrasts, she equally often transforms surfaces into optical space, creating spatial illusions.

Rolf Müller, Munich

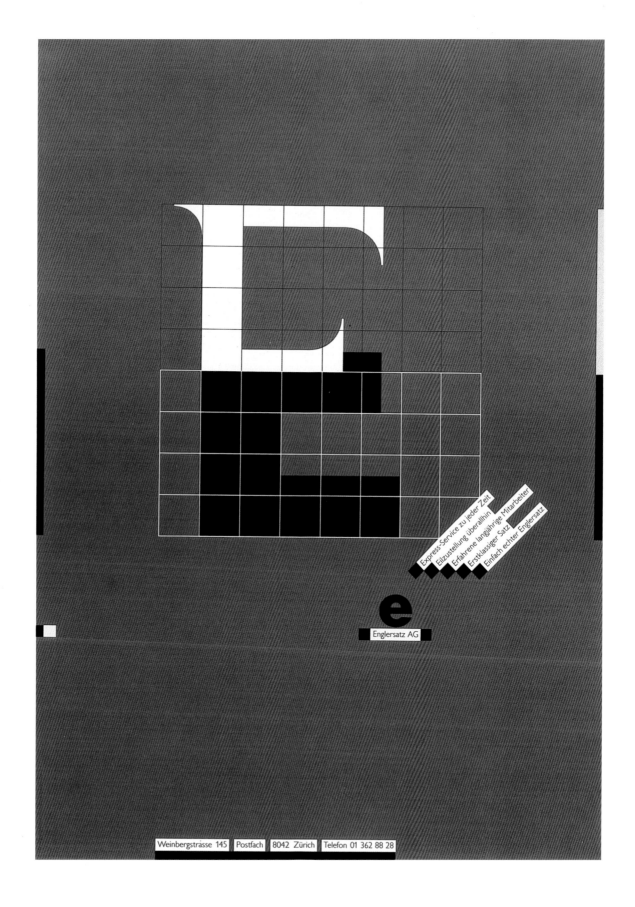

Express-Service zu jeder Zeit
Eilzustellung überallhin
Erfahrene langjährige Mitarbeiter
Erstklassiger Satz
Einfach echter Englersatz

e

Englersatz AG

Weinbergstrasse 145 | Postfach | 8042 Zürich | Telefon 01 362 88 28

Plakat
Poster
R. Tissi

STRAUHOF

Städtische Galerie
zum Strauhof
Augustinergasse 9
8001 Zürich

Serien
Variationen
Zyklen

**Ausstellung
vom 21. August bis
3. Oktober 1981**

Geöffnet:
Dienstag bis Freitag 10-18 Uhr
Donnerstag 10-21 Uhr
Samstag 10-16 Uhr
Sonntag und Montag geschlossen

**Max Bill
Margret Büsser
Ellen Classen**

**Christoph Fierz
Hans Gantert
Bruno Gentinetta**

**H. R. Giger
Emil Häfelin
Werner Hartmann**

**Waltraut Huth-Rössler
Joa Iselin
Peter König**

**Richard P. Lohse
H. R. Lutz
Peter Meister**

**Irene von Moos
Müller-Emil
Rolf Naghel**

**Hugo Schuhmacher
Carlos Teijelo
Annemarie Thummel**

Plakat
Poster
S. Odermatt

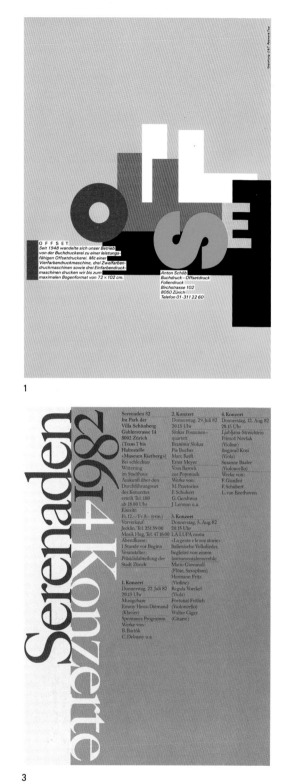

1

2

3

4

1, 2
Mappenumschläge
Covers of folders
R. Tissi

3, 4
Plakate
Posters
S. Odermatt

Paul Rand   **Paul Rand**

«Paul Rand ist gleichermassen Idealist und Realist, einer, der die Sprache des Dichters und die des Geschäftsmannes spricht. Sachzwang und Funktion gibt es für ihn . . . doch seine Phantasie ist grenzenlos.»
L. Moholy-Nagy

«Visuelle Kommunikation jeglicher Art, ob Werbung oder Information, vom gedruckten Programm bis zur Geburtsanzeige, sollte als die Verquickung von Form und Funktion gesehen werden: als die Vereinigung des Schönen mit dem Nützlichen. Vorlage, Kunst und Typografie sollten als lebendiges Ganzes gesehen werden; jedes Element ist gesamthaft eingebunden, in Harmonie mit dem Übergeordneten und wesentlich für die Umsetzung einer Idee. Wie ein Taschenspieler zeigt der Designer seine Fähigkeiten, indem er die Elemente in einem vorgegebenen Raum anordnet. Ob es sich bei diesem vorgegebenen Raum nun um Werbung, Zeitschriften, Bücher, Formulare, Verpackungen, Industrieerzeugnisse, Zeichen oder Fernsehprogramme handelt: Die Kriterien bleiben dieselben.»
(Aus «A Designer's Art», von Paul Rand. Mit freundlicher Genehmigung des Autors).

''Paul Rand is an idealist and a realist, one who uses the language of the poet and the businessman. He thinks in terms of need and function . . . but his fantasy is boundless.''
L. Moholy-Nagy

''Visual communications of any kind, whether persuasive or informative, from billboards to birth announcements, should be seen as the embodiment of form and function: the integration of the beautiful and the useful. Copy, art, and typography should be seen as a living entity; each element integrally related, in harmony with the whole, and essential to the execution of an idea. Like a juggler, the designer demonstrates his skills by manipulating these ingredients in a given space. Whether this space takes the form of advertisements, periodicals, books, printed forms, packages, industrial products, signs, or television billboards, the criteria are the same.''
(From ''A Designer's Art'' by Paul Rand, with the kind permission of the author.)

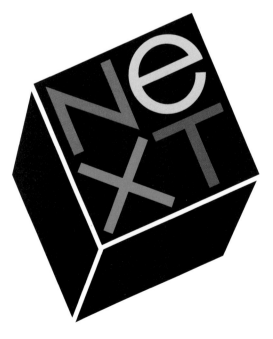

Firmenzeichen
Trademark

Westinghouse Annual Report

Jahresbericht
Annual report

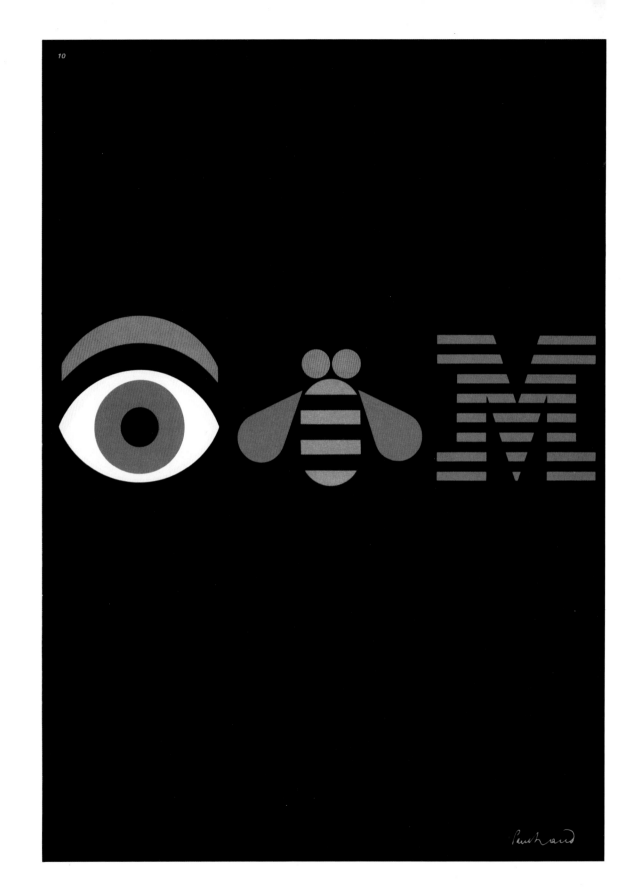

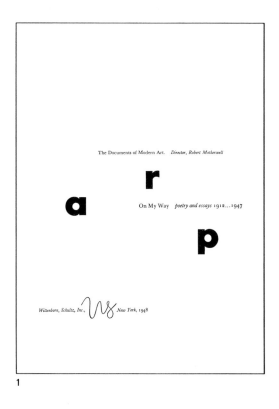

1

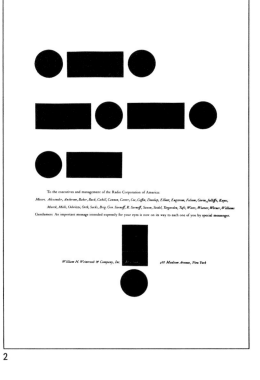

2

3

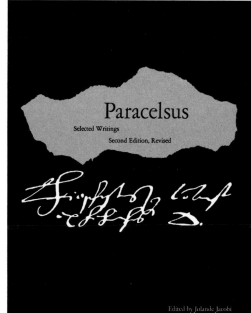

4

1
Titelseite
Title page

2
Inserat
Advertisement

3
Signet
Mark

4
Buchumschlag
Book cover

Heinz Waibl

Heinz Waibl

Lettern bedeuten für einen grafisch Kommunizierenden auf jeder Ebene seiner Tätigkeit eine Einschränkung, denn er muss einerseits eine systematische Analyse vornehmen, anderseits versuchen, diese Lettern auf kreative Art einzusetzen.

Ähnlich wie der Schriftsteller, der sich neben Grammatik und Syntax auch mit Wörtern und ihrem historischen Bedeutungswandel auseinanderzusetzen hat, muss sich auch der Grafikdesigner unermüdlich mit jedem Typensatz beschäftigen, muss seine Merkmale untersuchen und neue Verwendungsmöglichkeiten finden.

Sein unablässiges Schaffen unterliegt dabei zwei Lehrsätzen; einer wird von den Gesetzen des Schreibens bestimmt, der andere stammt von Stanley Morrison: «Soll ein neues Schriftbild Erfolg haben, muss es gut genug sein, um nur von wenigen überhaupt als neu erkannt zu werden.» Diese Aussage illustriert, wie konservativ der Verbraucher und Konsument ist.

Von diesen beiden Grundsätzen lasse ich mich ständig leiten, ob ich nun von Hand zeichne oder mich eines ruhigen mechanischen Hilfsmittels bediene.

Ich habe von Max Huber gelernt, einem grossen Meister, der immer noch mit fester Hand irgendeinen Letternsatz in 7-Punkt-Bodoni zeichnen kann, einem grossen Freund auch, der mir den Wunsch nach innovativem Arbeiten mitgegeben hat, nach einer Art poetischer Freiheit, die sowohl Substanz als auch Form beinhaltet, was dem Stil sehr nahekommt.

Types are a restriction for a graphic communicator at all stages of his work, as he has to carry on a systematic analysis while trying to use them creatively.

In the same way as a writer has to deal with words, as well as grammar and syntax, and their meanings throughout their historical evolution, so must a graphic designer tirelessly go over each set of types, study their features, invent new uses for them.

This continuous activity of his is subject to two rules: one determined by the laws of writing, the other, established by Stanley Morison, according to whom, ''for a new set of types to be successful it must be good enough not to be recognized as new but by a few'', which illustrates the conservative character of the user-consumer.

These two principles are my constant concern whether I am drawing by hand or using a silent, steady, mechanical device.

I have learnt from Max Huber, a great master who still shows a firm hand in drawing any ''body type'' in 7-point Bodoni, and a great friend who has instilled into me a taste for the innovative touch, for a sort of poetic licence involving substance and form which comes to be close to style.

Wortmarke
Logotype

Type La tipografia nel filtro ottico.
È bene distinguere subito le diverse aree della tipografia che sono nate da specifiche applicazioni, onde evitare di costringere questa immensa materia ad un giudizio circoscritto e limitativo.

Innanzi tutto la tipografia è nata per farsi leggere attraverso la spogliazione del segno dalla sua forma visiva, codificando le lettere ed estraendone il significato. La parola scritta, in questo caso, non viene ricordata come immagine, ma rimane solo parola che si realizza come idea.

Così è la tipografia per la pagina del libro o del giornale, dove il vuoto e il pieno delle lettere, la giustezza o la lunghezza della riga, il corpo o la grandezza del carattere, l'interlineatura o lo spazio tra le righe, i margini della pagina, concorrono a fornire quegli ingredienti di base che rendono facile ed invitante la lettura.

Ma i miei interessi professionali, estetici e creativi, si sono sempre indirizzati, sperimentalmente, verso una tipografia di alto richiamo visivo al servizio della comunicazione in ambiente saturo di segni, come per esempio, il settore della pubblicità, dove le frasi sono state scelte più brevi e incisive, assumendo talvolta il ruolo di figurazione.

Da un pò di tempo la riga tipografica ha perso la sua «periodicità meccanica» perchè condizionata dalla foto-composizione che regola le distanze alfabetiche con accorgimenti microvisivi irregolari tali da non essere percepiti dall'occhio umano, e queste libertà ottiche hanno poi influito nei macrosegni ad alterare le forze spaziali quando esse fanno sentire le «differenze» che si rincorrono nell'area del campo di lettura, aumentando la tensione formale e l'intensità del significato della parola.

In questi ultimi anni è stato un fiorire di nuovi alfabeti che non possiedono più il veto della difficile lettura perchè attraverso le nostre continue esperienze di nuovi segni, logotipi, insegne, espressioni grafiche libere, l'occhio ha acquistato una maggiore velocità interpretativa alla lettura.

Quando nel 1964 disegnai per la prima volta il carattere «Magnetic» ispirato ai numeri IBM, stampati con inchiostri magnetici, ebbi il dubbio della poca leggibilità (per quanto io li avessi usati per la copertina di «Pubblicità in Italia» 1964-65) ma nel 1966 questi caratteri furono ripresi in America e trasferiti in fotocomposizione e applicati subito alla titolazione avveniristica in migliaia di pubblicazioni.

La mia personale ricerca che man mano si è sviluppata dal 1953 in questo settore è stata la proiezione di segni alfabetici attraverso filtri ottici, per ottenere le sensazioni come «distanza drammatica». Il segno, con queste tecniche, diventa «fisico» non per la materia ma per la carica di spinte e controspinte che fanno sì che l'occhio umano veda attraverso emozione e sollecitazione che creano valori traumatici e rubano lo sguardo facendo sentire un disagio percettivo espresso in ansia.

Non è stata questa ricerca il bisogno del nuovo a tutti i costi, ma l'analisi della situazione della lettura tipografica influenzata dalla velocità meccanica dei mezzi di locomozione, o da interferenze di superfici trasparenti nelle architetture, o da ricuperi di forme riflesse in superfici curvate e speculari.

Chiunque analizzi il futuro della comunicazione scritta non può non sgomentarsi davanti all'enorme, irrazionale, enfatico consumo di simboli. Valanghe di segni, immagini e illustrazioni, assorbono circa il 70% dello spazio nei mass-media togliendoci l'esercizio del controllo sui processi di memoria e abituando la nostra mente ad una superficiale osservazione.

L'area operativa della pubblicità sta diventando sempre più vasta e lo sforzo creativo di specialisti non riesce ormai a produrre, per due prodotti similari, quanto basta per differenziarli. In questo mondo di immagini, che sta raggiungendo valori ipertrofici, si impone la ricerca di nuovi valori segnici, fisici e costruttivi.

Anche la grafica moderna, a causa della sua estrema semplificazione, rischia una unificazione dei segni che porta ineluttabilmente alla similarità. Si è scritto che nel futuro l'immagine soppianterà anche la parola scritta, ma si può affermare oggi che la tipografia può essere il soggetto e può sostituire la figurazione quando applica l'espressività dinamica o quando la stessa lettera, ingrandita, diventa antropometrica per ricordare con le sue sinuosità il corpo umano.

Nell'800 la tipografia nella pubblicità entrava come sostegno alla figurazione e ne occupava lo spazio lasciato libero; ora la tipografia è immagine violenta per colore e tridimensionalità, con la funzione di fermare il lettore-pedone o l'automobilista nei canali del traffico cittadino.

Oggi le città hanno due architetture, una fisica e l'altra di parole stampate e di neon; forse, parlare di prospettiva, è improprio, bisogna parlare di proiettiva o di «tensione imaginativa» dove l'uomo vive la sua vita diurna e notturna nei canali del flusso viario.

Il graphic-designer, entrando in questi problemi, si appoggia ad una cultura scientifico-visiva: indaga lo spazio che lo attornia e che si rivela come una espansione radiale.

Fino a qualche anno fa la grafica moderna si amministrava su moduli, ricercava l'ordine, l'armonia nella composizione, sfociando in un concetto statico. Ora, invece, non cerca l'equilibrio, la stabilità, ma un campo di sollecitazioni visive in continua trasformazione che rinvigoriscono di volta in volta le possibilità e le qualità del suo segno.

Che cos'è una distorsione se non l'infiltrarsi di uno spirito «sperimentale» verso la ricerca di aspetti alterati, decomposti, astratti, e logicamente autonomi; che cos'è la tensione, se non la lettura sull'arco fisico del segno degli elementi della quarta dimensione psicofisica, un alcaloide per la lettura di movimenti virtuali che aumentano l'intensità del significato...

Type è una selezione di esempi, alcuni già applicati, altri in riserva, di tutto ciò che si può ottenere vedendo «oltre» lo sguardo, un lavoro travagliato ma libero, inventivo, paradossale, inspiegabile e razionalissimo, uno spettacolo di idee che nutrono la fantasia.

Queste sperimentazioni, pubblicate in tutte le riviste grafiche del mondo hanno, alla fine, influenzato altre grafiche anche in altri paesi. Mi sembra opportuno, ora, mostrarle qui per indicare una cultura della visione aperta al miglioramento intellettivo di tutta la grafica che vuole chiamarsi moderna.

Franco Grignani 15 marzo 1984

Quanta
via Fatebenefratelli 15 20121 Milano

1987

NAVA milano spa

1

1 DOMENICA 2 LUNEDI
3 MARTEDI MERCOL
8 DOME
NICA
15 DOMENI
CA
22 DOMEN
ICA

NAVA milano spa

2

Agosto 1987 August

1 SABATO 2 DOMENICA
3 LUNEDI 4 MARTEDI
5 MERCOLEDI 6 GIOVE
DI 7 VENERDI 8 SABA
TO 9 DOMENICA 10 LU
NEDI 11 MARTEDI 12 M
ERCOLEDI 13 GIOVEDI
14 VENERDI 15 SABAT
O 16 DOMENICA 17 LU
NEDI 18 MARTEDI 19 M
ERCOLEDI 20 GIOVEDI
21 VENERDI 22 SABAT
O 23 DOMENICA 24 LU
NEDI 25 MARTEDI 26
MERCOLEDI 27 GIOVE
DI 28 VENERDI 29 SAB
ATO 30 DOMENICA 31
LUNEDI

NAVA milano spa

3

Settembre 1987 September

1 MARTEDI 2 MERCOLEDI
3 GIOVEDI 4 VENERDI 5
SABATO 6 DOMENICA 7
LUNEDI 8 MARTEDI 9 M
ERCOLEDI 10 GIOVEDI 11
VENERDI 12 SABATO 13
DOMENICA 14 LUNEDI
15 MARTEDI 16 MERCOL
EDI 17 GIOVEDI 18 VENE
RDI 19 SABATO 20 DOM
ENICA 21 LUNEDI 22 MA
RTEDI 23 MERCOLEDI 24
GIOVEDI 25 VENERDI 26
SABATO 27 DOMENICA
28 LUNEDI 29 MARTEDI
30 MERCOLEDI

NAVA milano spa

4

1-4
Kalenderblätter
Calendar sheets

S Madre di Dio

Thursday   January
Jeudi   Janvier
Giovedi Gennaio   1
Donnerstag Januar
Jueves   Enero

1

1

1–5
Kalenderblätter
Calendar sheets

2   3   4   5

Wolfgang Weingart
Der Typografie-Unterricht für die
Weiterbildungsklassen an der Schule für
Gestaltung in Basel, Schweiz

Wolfgang Weingart
The Typography Education for advanced
studies at the Basel School of Design,
Switzerland

Wie kann eine Schule heute, morgen und in
absehbarer Zukunft junge Menschen aus-
oder weiterbilden, ohne dass diese in den
Sog beruflicher Pfuscherei und rücksichts-
losen Profitdenkens geraten und schliesslich
von unaufhörlicher Hastigkeit erdrückt werden?

Das Quantitative und das zunehmende
Chaos unserer Zeit in Schule, Ausbildung
oder Weiterbildung und Praxis zu verringern
oder wenn möglich zu beseitigen ist für den
Typografieunterricht an der Schule für
Gestaltung Basel ein hochgestecktes Ziel.
Dieses Ziel bedeutet nichts anderes, als das
einzelne Individuum wieder in eine direkte
Beziehung zum eigenen Machen zurückzu-
führen. Wir versuchen, diese Vorstellungen
in bescheidenem Masse zu verwirklichen.

In der Typografiewerkstatt wurde der Kreis
geschlossen: Neben klassischem Handsatz
mit verschiedenen Testandruckpressen,
mit einer professionellen Reproduktions-
abteilung für die lithografische Weiterverar-
beitung sowie einem stufenlosen Normal-
papierkopiergerät finden sich mehrere
Macintosh-Computer mit ImageWriter und
LaserWriter. Alle Einrichtungen und Geräte
werden in den Entwurfsunterricht einbezo-
gen. Ob Handpressenabzug, Film, Kopie
oder Computerausdruck – alle Einzelent-
würfe lassen sich gestalterisch kombinieren
und zu einer spannungsreichen Einheit ver-
binden.

Nur fundierte Kenntnisse der elementarsten
und klassischen Gestaltungsgrundlagen
machen es möglich, in unterschiedlichster
Weise gestalterische Probleme anzugehen
und zu realisieren. Durch den aktuellen Einbe-
zug des Computers in den Basler Typografie-
unterricht lautet der Anspruch heute und
in Zukunft: Wer die faszinierenden Möglichkeiten des Computers in den Arbeitsalltag
einbeziehen möchte, bedarf einer konsequenten, gründlichen und klassischen Grund-
ausbildung als Gestalter.

How can a college educate and train young
people today, tomorrow and in the foresee-
able future without letting them fall into the
mire of professional half-measures and
heedless profit-seeking, finally to be crushed
by incessant deadline pressure?

One of the highest aims of the Typographical
Studies department of the Basle School of
Design is to reduce or, where possible, elimi-
nate the great and increasing chaos of our
times in education and training and, eventu-
ally, in professional practice. This aim means
nothing less than leading the individual back
into a direct relationship with his own work.
We try to put these ideas into practice to a
modest extent.

In the typographical workshop the circle is
closed: in addition to traditional handsetting
and proofing on a variety of test presses,
with a professional repro department for
litho processing and an enlarging and reducing plain-paper photocopier, there are
several Macintosh computers equipped with
ImageWriters and LaserWriters. All of these
installations and varieties of equipment are
put to use in design classes. Whether they
are in the form of hand-press proofs,
exposed on film, photocopied or printed out
from the computer, all individual exercises
can be combined in the design process to
make a vital unity.

Only a well-grounded knowledge of the most
elementary and traditional basic factors of
design makes it possible to approach and
solve design problems in a versatile manner.
The present inclusion of the computer in
typographical studies at Basle has given us
a watchword for today and the future: whoever wishes to bring the fascinating possibilities of the computer into everyday work
first needs a consistent, fundamental and
traditional basic education as a designer.

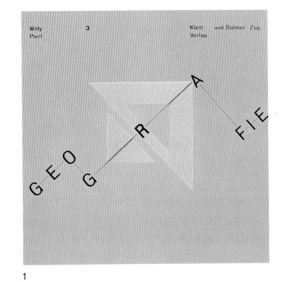

1

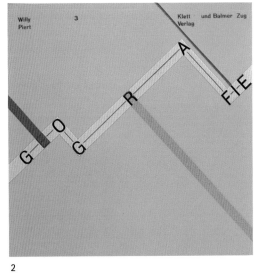

2

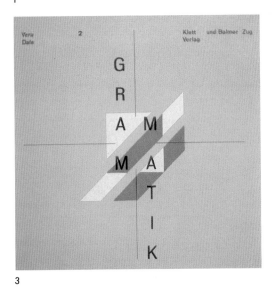

3

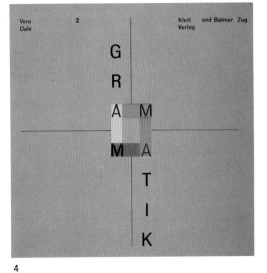

4

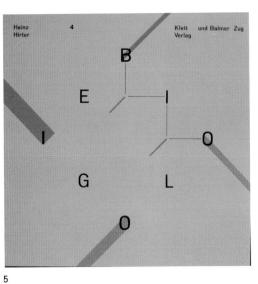

5

6

1– 6
Buchumschläge
Book jackets
Heinz Hiltbrunner
Schule für Gestaltung
Basel
Basel School of Design

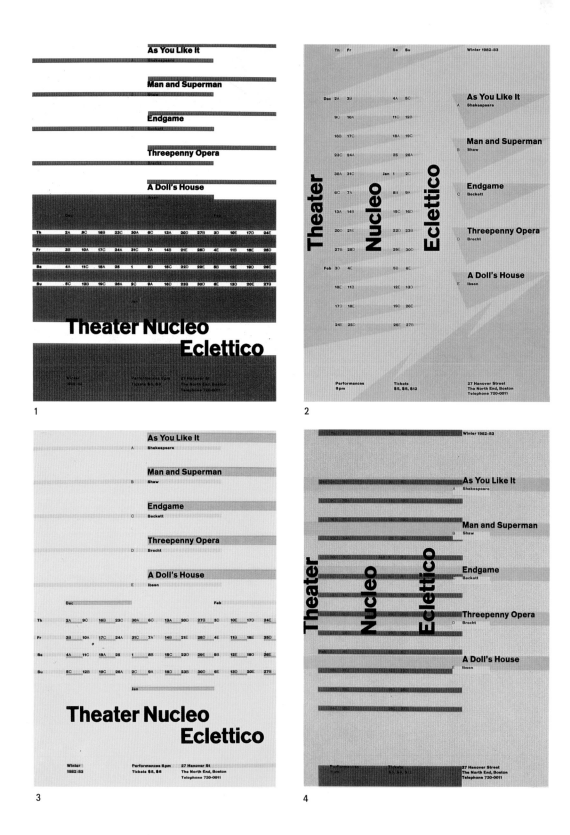

1-4
Plakate
Posters
Lorrain Ferguson
Schule für Gestaltung
Basel
Basel School of Design

Mustermesse Basel
Rundhofgebäude/Halle 10

KUNST KREDIT 1980/81

Ausstellung
25. Juli bis 16. August 1981

Öffnungszeiten:
Täglich 10–12 und 14–18 Uhr
Samstag 1. August geschlossen

Führungen: Dienstag und Freitag 20–22 Uhr

Wettbewerbe, Aufträge und Ankäufe
des Staatlichen Kunstkredits.

Eintritt
frei

Plakat
Poster
Wolfgang Weingart

Typo-Bücher
Eine kleine Auswahl von Publikationen für
den typografischen Gestalter

Typography-Books
A small selection of publications for
designers

Typografie (d, e)
Otl Aicher,
Verlag ernst & sohn,
Berlin, 1988

**Technische Grundlagen zur
Satzherstellung** (d)
Hans-Rudolf Bosshard,
Verlag des Bildungsverbandes
Schweizerischer Typografen,
Bern, Schweiz, 1980

**Typographic Design;
Form and Communication** (e)
Carter/Day/Meggs,
Van Nostrand Reinhold Company,
New York, USA, 1985

Designing with type (e)
James Craig,
Watson-Guptill Publications, New York,
Pitman Publishing, London, 1980

Kompendium für Alphabeten (d und e)
Karl Gerstner,
Verlag A. Niggli, Teufen, Schweiz, 1972 (d)
MIT Press, Chicago, USA (e)

Igarashi Alphabets (d, e, f)
Takenobu Igarashi,
ABC Verlag,
Zürich, Schweiz, 1987

Typo (d)
Hans-Rudolf Lutz,
Verlag Hans-Rudolf Lutz,
Zürich, Schweiz, 1987

**Die Geschichte der visuellen
Kommunikation** (d, e)
J. Müller-Brockmann
Verlag A. Niggli
Teufen, Schweiz, 1986

Typographie (d)
Emil Ruder,
Verlag Arthur Niggli,
Teufen, Schweiz, 1967/1988

Typography Today (e, j)
Helmut Schmid,
IDEA Special Issue,
Seibundo Skinkosha, Publishing Co. Ltd.,
Tokio, Japan, 1980

The Visible Word (e)
Herbert Spencer,
Lund Humphries,
London, England, 1969

Pioneers of modern typography (e)
Herbert Spencer, MIT Press,
Cambridge, MA, USA, 1983

The Liberated Page (e)
Herbert Spencer,
Bedford Press,
San Francisco, CA, USA, 1987

Legibility of Print (e)
Miles A. Tinker,
The Iowa State University Press,
Ames, Iowa, USA, 1969

Die Neue Typographie (d)
Jan Tschichold,
Verlag Brinkmann & Bose,
Berlin, 1928/1987

d = deutsch / German
e = englisch / English
j = japanisch / Japanese
f = französisch / French